MERCHANT FLEETS

MERCHANT FLEETS

Reprinted and updated 1990

British Library Cataloguing Publication Data

Haws, Duncan
   Merchant Fleets 8
   Pacific Steam Navigation Co.
   1. Merchant Marine — History
   1. Title

   ISBN 0 946378 03 7

TEXT photoset in 9 on 10pt Times
by C. I. Thomas and Sons (Haverfordwest) Ltd.,
Merlins Bridge, Haverfordwest, Dyfed.
TCL Publications, 1 Meadowbank, Hereford HR1 2ST.

Contents

Introduction

It is hard to conceive a more adventurous and hazardous undertaking than that of William Wheelwright when he decided upon steamer services not from Liverpool or from London but out of Valparaiso in the young Republic of Chile. The mere logistics of coal, crewing, overhauls and machinery breakdown multiplied by the length of the coastline and its virtual lack of facilities must have placed his venture in the same sceptical category of comment as today's 'It's easier to put a man on the moon.'

Not content with the need to open up the whole of the under charted west coast of South America (as witness the number of hulks that became the necessary coal depots at his ports of call) William Wheelwright introduced connecting mail services from Liverpool. To cater for local passenger needs he created that new breed of vessel: the coastal passenger liner. These beautiful and versatile ships served a mileage equivalent to a transatlantic crossing with clocklike punctuality.

It was progressively inevitable that South American Governments would emerge eventually to control their own coastal shipping and that the aeroplane would serve passenger needs but it is, nevertheless, a matter of much sadness that the name of the Pacific Steam Navigation Company no longer plies the South American waters.

May I convey my appreciation for all his help to John E. Lingwood, J.P., Historical Archivist, P.S.N.C., Liverpool, now retired; to the Furness Withy Group Public Relations Department and to the Shipping Information Services of Lloyds Register. With their generous assistance many details have been added and facts verified.

Duncan Haws

Burwash. December 1985.

Explanatory Notes

1 Company histories are arranged chronologically.

2 The ships owned are listed virtually chronologically except that sister ships are grouped together even when the period of their building covers more than one year.

3 Tonnage: the method of calculating tonnage has changed several times since 1830 and very few ships kept their initial tonnage. The gross and net tonnages shown are generally those recorded when the ship first entered service.

4 Dimensions: unless recorded as 'overall' the figures given are the registered dimensions between perpendiculars.

5 The speed given is service speed. This could vary according to route and ports of call.

6 Abbreviations: to assist all readers as few as possible have been used —

Apr	*April*	g	*Gross*
Aug	*August*	GP	*Goal post masts*
BHP	*Brake horse power*	GRT	*Gross registered tonnage*
Blr	*boiler*	**H**	*Hull*
B	*Built*	HP	*Horse power/High pressure*
B	*Bridgedeck*	IHP	*Indicated horse power*
cabin	*Cabin class*	in	*Inch(es)*
cm	*Centimetres*	Jan	*January*
cu m	*Cubic metres*	K.K.	*Kabusiki Kaisya*
cu ft	*Cubic feet*	kts	*Knots*
Cyl(s)	*Cylinder(s)*	lb	*Pound(s)*
D	*Dimensions*	LP	*Low Pressure*
dbl	*Double*	m	*Metre*
Dec	*December*	Mar	*March*
Dft	*Draught/draft*	mm	*Millimetres*
diam	*Diameter*	MP	*Medium pressure*
disp	*Displacement*	mph	*Miles per hour*
dwt	*Dead weight*	n	*Net*
E	*East*	N	*North*
E	*Engine*	NHP	*Nominal horse power*
exp	*expansion*	Nov	*November*
F	*Forecastle*	oa	*Overall*
Feb	*February*	obb	*over bulbous bow*
ft	*Feet*	Oct	*October*
fwd	*Forward*	Pad	*Paddle*

P	*Passengers*	Sept	*September*
P	*Poop*	sgl	*Single*
Prom	*Promenade*	SHP	*Shaft horse power*
Q	*Quarterdeck*	Stm	*Steam*
quad	*Quadruple/four*	Stm P	*Steam pressure*
refrig	*Refrigerated*	SV	*Sailing vessel*
reg	*Registered*	T	*Tons*
RHP	*Registered horse power*	TEU	*Twenty foot equivalent units*
rpm	*Revolutions per minute*	tpl	*Triple/three*
S	*South*	tst	*tourist*
S.SA	*Stroke, Sgl acting*	tw	*Twin/two*
S.DA	*stroke, Dbl acting*	W	*West*
scr	*Screw*		

7 The technical data follows the same pattern throughout —

B (built; **T** (tons), g (gross), n (net), dwt (dead weight). **Dim** (dimensions) oa (overall) length x breadth x depth; *Dft:* (draught). **Eng** (engine) Pad (Paddle), sgl (single) dbl (double), scr (screw); Cyls: (cylinders); IHP, NHP, SHP, BHP, RHP, HP; Boilers; *Stm P:* (steam pressure) lb (pounds); kts (knots); By (engine builder). **H** (hull details); *Coal, Cargo; Pass;* (passengers), 1st (first class), 2nd (second class), 3rd (third class), tst (tourist class); Crew.

SOUTH AMERICA

P.S.N.C.

HISTORY

1798 Mar 18: William Wheelwright, son of a Lincolnshire master mariner, was born at Newbury Port, Massachusetts, USA and was educated at Phillips Academy, Andover, Mass.

1814 William Wheelwright went to sea as a cabin boy, aged 16, aboard a family ship.

1817 Having served his apprenticeship aboard sailing brigs out of New Orleans William Wheelwright achieved his first command at the age of 19.

1823 His ship, the barque *Rising Empire*, (owned by William Bartlett) was wrecked at the mouth of the River Plate off the Argentine coast. As a result he shipped out of Beunos Aires as a seaman for Valparaiso. There he transhipped and arrived at Guayaquil, Ecuador, where he set up business as a ship broker and chandler, even becoming US Consul at the port.

1828 Wheelwright travelled back to Newbury Port and married Martha Bell taking her back with him via Panama to Guayaquil. There he found his business in ruins with heavy debts of almost $100,000. As a result the couple moved south back to Valparaiso, a port which had fascinated the young man because of its proximity to the capital of Chile, Santiago. The first vessel owned by him was the schooner *Fourth of July* with which he traded northwards up the coast. It was clear not only to William Wheelwright but also to the Chilean Government that the coastal seaway offered the country's best communication. Roads were non existent and the building of them quite impractical. Trade flowed from port to port and any roadways merely funnelled into them. The one inhibiting vagary was the wind and the frequent lack of it. Steam propulsion offered a solution and promised a regularity of service which could be of great benefit to both the land based industries and to the farmers.

1835 Aug 5: The Government of Chile granted Wheelwright, by decree, the exclusive rights to steam navigation in Chilean waters for a period of 10 years. They insisted that he should begin his steamer services within two years but in the event the project was to take five more years to mature.

1836 June 18: Peruvian merchants became interested in the steam concept; at a meeting convened there by the British Consul General a committee was formed to study Wheelwright's proposals. Nov 8: Back in Santiago a meeting chaired there by the British Consul General recommended the urgent formation of a company to raise the capital to build the envisaged steamships. Wheelwright set off for the United States to seek support but failed and continued on to Britain.

1837 Aug 4: The Chilean decree of 1835 lapsed but, impressed with the attempts being made, power of attorney was granted which deleted the two year implementation clause. Providentially for Wheelwright the British Government were themselves anxious to expand trade to the west coast of South America. A voyage under sail to Valparaiso took at least four months, so a route southwards over Panama with connecting steamers was obviously attractive. Lord Abinger's son the Hon. Peter Scarlett had written a treatise advocating a railway across the Isthmus to connect an

Atlantic terminal with a Pacific distribution port capable of feeding steamers that could sail south, north or even eastwards. Baron Friedrich von Humboldt (1769-1859) had also advocated building a ship canal across the 50 mile isthmus.

1838 Sept 27: The Pacific Steam Navigation Company Limited finally came into being at 5 Barge Yard, Bucklesbury, London. The share capital was £250,000 of 5,000 shares of £50 each with 1,000 reserved for South American investors. Mr. George Brown was appointed the first Chairman; he was also a founding director of the Royal Mail Steam Packet Company so that the interlinking fortunes of the two concerns were conjoined from their very start. At this stage the house flag had Chile's White Star in place of the crown. William Wheelwright's position was that of the resident director at Valparaiso where he had a number of other business interests.

Initial interest was slow; in fact the only investors were the Directors whose qualifying shares produced £5,000. The granting of the Royal Charter was awaited by investors as the seal of approval of the Government. A full eighteen months was to pass before this was to be granted and when it was the Crown of England replaced the White Star at the centre of the house flag. In the meantime plans to commence services proceeded. Wheelwright's proposition had been for three iron hulled steamers of 700 tons plus a fourth in reserve; he pointed out that the lack of facilities in South America necessitated the reserve steamer.

1839 Aug 31: Orders for two ships were placed with Thomas Wilson & Co, Liverpool. However, because of the delay over the Royal Charter the Board, in Wheelwright's absence, cancelled the order. Wheelwright's adamant intervention led to the re-issuing of the tenders but Thomas Wilson would have nothing to do with this embryonic, under-capitalised, Chilean based concern. Oct 10: The order went to Curling and Young, London, but for ships with wooden not iron hulls despite the opposition of William Wheelwright.

1840 Jan: The Royal Charter was granted at long last. This set the scene fair for the development of the company. In the following month on Feb 17 George Peacock was appointed the company's first Captain. Wheelwright was now appointed Chief Superintendent of the Company, his salary was £1,400 per annum, and Peacock was made Second Superintendent with responsibility for operating the two ships.

1840 In preparation for the Chilean coastal services the wooden sailing ship *Elizabeth* was purchased and loaded with coal. Her crew refused to sail her saying that she was unseaworthy for Cape Horn and their view was confirmed when the vessel was inspected by William Wheelwright. To replace her the wooden barque *Portsea* was acquired, loaded with the coal, and sent to Valparaiso where she was hulked. Two other coal hulks joined her at Valparaiso they were the *Cecilia* and *Jasper*.

Apr 18: *Peru* (I) launched.

Apr 21: *Chile* (I) launched.

Jun 27: *Chile* left Falmouth for Valparaiso and on July 15 *Peru* followed from Plymouth; both had a rendez-vous in the Straits of Magellan. The plan was for both vessels to steam round the headland into Valparaiso Bay together and to berth simultaneously. The whole event was however overshadowed by Cunard's *Britannia* which entered service at the same time.

Oct 16: To a tumultuous welcome both ships arrived. The voyage time was 52 days for the 8,600 miles.

Oct 25: *Peru* opened the service between Valparaiso - Callao (Peru)

1841-2 Although the service was maintained problems were manifest not least being the difficulty in assuring adequate supplies of coal. At one stage the steamers had to be laid up for three months because of a lack of it.

1843 Wheelwright returned to London where he was dismissed on Oct 5, at a Board meeting, for 'bad management'. In response he circultated his report to the shareholders who in return voted for the removal of his accusers, except George Brown, and his return to the Board as Joint Managing Director. The main shareholders were Liverpool merchants, and the head office of the company was moved to that city. Because of his need to return to Valparaiso another Joint Managing Director was appointed for the British end of the enterprise. He was William Just of the Aberdeen and London S.S. Co. Wheelwright's own powers were expanded to include not only Chile but also Peru, Ecuador, Colombia and Panama. Nevertheless at this point in time, out of a capital of £94,000, £72,000 had been lost. *Valdivia* (I) was delivered.

1846 *Ecuador* (I) took up station at Callao and extended the Valparaiso service via Guayaquil to Panama. This in turn connected with the Royal Mail S P Co's service Southampton-Colon to create the Panama-Overland route to Valparaiso which could be reached in 40 days in place of the four months via Cape Horn. Later in the year *New Granada* arrived to join *Ecuador* at Callao.

1847 The hulk *Cecilia* was lost and replaced by *Queen of The Ocean*.

1849 *Bolivia* (I) a third unit of the *Chile* class was delivered.

1850 Sept: The Board meeting at Liverpool declared a 10% dividend.

1851 The growth of trading along the coast plus a mail contract enabled PSNC to order, at a cost of £140,000, four ships with which to replace the tiny *Chile* and *Peru*, whose wooden hulls were only guaranteed for 12 years, and to augment *Bolivia*. Of the four *Santiago* (I) and *Lima* (I) were delivered. *Ecuador* (I) was wrecked at Coquimbo.

1852 *Quito* (I) and *Bogota* (I) were delivered. *Chile* (I) was sold but *Peru* (I) went aground and became a total loss. With the four new steamers PSNC maintained a fortnightly service between Valparaiso and Panama and were granted the British Government mail contract.

1853 The company's smaller coastal vessels were first obliged to make the long journey out from Britain to Valparaiso. This hazardous undertaking carried penalties and in this year *Perlita* and *Osprey* were both lost on their delivery voyages. In addition *Quito* (I) was wrecked on the coast and the hulk *Hope* was lost.

1854 *Panama* (I) and *Prince of Wales* entered PSNC service. Unfortunately *Panama* was lost on her maiden voyage after striking a rock. The Panama Railway across the isthmus was completed to open a "through" route to the west coast of South America.

1856 The compound engine was invented and PSNC were the first to install this new economic machinery. *Valparaiso* (I) and *Inca* (I) both had the direct acting variety. It was to be 14 years before other shipowners commenced regularly to install compound engines. Alfred Holt being the foremost.

1857 *Santiago* (I) was sold but *Valdivia* (I) was lost.

1858 *Callao* (I), sister of *Valparaiso*, delivered. *Cloda* purchased.

1859 *Prince of Wales* was wrecked on the coast of Chile and *Anne* was acquired locally as a replacement. The island of Morro in Panama Bay was acquired and became 'North Station' with workshops and stores.

1860 *San Carlos, Guayaquil* and *Peruano* were delivered. *Morro* (I) became the company tender at Panama. New hulks were *Constitution* and *Lord Hungerford*, which foundered en route. At the end of the company's first 20 years the PSNC fleet comprised of twelve steamers.

Bolivia (I), *Lima* (I), *Bogota* (I), *Inca* (I), *Valparaiso* (I), *Callao* (I), *Cloda, Anne, San Carlos, Guayaquil, Morro* (I) and *Peruano*.

1862 *Peru* (II) and *Talca* (I) joined the fleet.

1863 *Chile* (II) joined her sister ship *Peru*.

1864 *Anne* sold; at 344 gross tons she was too small in comparison with the new vessels entering service; but as a temporary replacement for the loss of *Prince of Wales* she had served five useful years with PSNC.

1865 The Charter of PSNC was amended to include the establishment of steamer services between the West Coast of South America and the River Plate, including the Falkland Islands, and 'such other ports or places in North and South America, and other foreign ports as the said company shall deem expedient.'

Cloda was lost off Huacho and *Quito* (II) was sold.

New additions were *Pacific, Santiago* (II), *Limena* and the American river-boat style *Favorita.*

1866 *Panama* (I), fourth and last of the *Pacific* class, was delivered and *Colon* was purchased locally to replace *Cloda.*

1867 In December at a special meeting of the shareholders it was agreed to commence a monthly service from Liverpool to Valparaiso via the Straits of Magellan. Five screw steamers were ordered and to meet this expansion the capital of the company was increased to £2,000,000. The reason for the decision arose from the continued refusal of the Panaman Railroad Co. to grant PSNC the same advantageous through rates that applied to cargo for USA ports.

1868 The new ships were yet to be commissioned but the company was anxious to begin the Liverpool-South America service. Accordingly on May 13 the paddle steamer *Pacific* left Valparaiso for Liverpool with 170 passengers thereby inaugurating the new venture. Her three sister vessles duly joined *Pacific* and sailings every six weeks followed. To this quartet fell the distinction of being the only compound paddle steamers on the transatlantic routes. The ports of call were Bordeaux - Lisbon - Cape Verde Islands - Rio-de Janeiro - Montevideo - Punta Arenas - Valparaiso. *Caldera* was commissioned but the important addition was *Magellan* (I), the first of the Liverpool-Valparaiso fleet.

1869 Whilst serving on the Liverpool-Valparaiso route *Santiago* (II) was wrecked in the Straits of Magellan on an uncharted rock, and the two year old *Arica* (I) went ashore and was lost.

The remaining three of the four sister screw steamers ordered in December 1867 began to come into service with the arrival of *Patagonia, Araucania* and *Cordillera.* Also delivered was the famous *John Elder*, the ship which PSNC named after the inventor of the compound engine which had revolutionised the economic viability of their coastal services. Ironically John Elder himself died before the commissioning of the ship named after him. *John Elder* also differed by being increased in length and breadth soon after construction. She had two funnels although initially, from the illustrations of the time, she appeared with one funnel.

1870 The Directors had decided to extend the Liverpool-Valparaiso service northwards to Callao via Arica and Mollendo and to increase the sailings to three per month. For the service four steamers *Atacama, Coquimbo, Valdivia* (II) and *Eten* (1871) were built. The smaller *Arequipa* (I) was also added and her arrival released *Guayaquil* for sale.

The first of two local steamers for the Callao berth was delivered, the *Haucho.* The eleven vessels ordered in the year constituted their, then, largest order placed for ships.

1871 *Iquique* followed *Huacho. Valparaiso* (I) was wrecked and *Favorita* destroyed by fire at Callao, while *Bogota* (I) struck a reef at Tarada. The significant event of the year was the arrival of the first group of a new class of ships for the Liverpool-Valparaiso-Callao through service. They were *Chimborazo, Cuzco, Garonne* and *Lusitania.*

Dec: Lusitania shed her propeller shortly after leaving Valparaiso. A caisson was built around the stern, pumped dry and the new screw fitted.

1872 A mail subsidy of £10,000 per annum was granted in support of a weekly service to Callao and the capital was increased to £3 million. At this time White Star Line made its short lived attempt to enter the market when, on October 5, their steamer *Republic* sailed for Valparaiso and Callao. The brand new steamer *Tacora*, racing against *Republic*, was lost on her maiden voyage, near to Montevideo.

1873 Jan 8: *Sorata* (I) took the first weekly sailing and carried the mails under a new contract. During a visit to London where he planned to reside, William Wheelwright, aged 75, died on Sept 26. By the end of the year the imposing trans-Atlantic fleet was complete and PSNC became, if one includes the coastal fleet, the largest steamship company in the world.

For ease of reference the composition of the company is recorded:

Atlantic fleet:

1869 *Magellan, Araucania, Cordillera, Patagonia, John Elder*

1871 *Chimborazo, Cuzco, Garonne, Lusitania*

1872 *Aconcagua, Corcovado, Sorata, Tacora*

1873 *Britannia, Cotopaxi, Galicia, Iberia, Illimani, Liguria, Potosi, Puno, Valparaiso.*

Coastal Fleet *Inca* (I), *Callao* (I), *San Carlos, Guayaquil, Morro* (I), *Peruano, Peru* (III), *Chile* (II), *Talca* (I), *Payta, Ecuador* (II), *Pacific, Limena, Supe, Atlas, Caldera, Atacama, Coquimbo, Valdivia* (II), *Eten, Arequipa* (I), *Huacho, Iquique, Santiago* (III), *Taboguilla, Santa Rosa, Colombia, Rimac, Truxillo, Baja, Ayacucho, Lima, Oroya* (I), *Islay, Tacna.*

Nevertheless PSNC had over-reached itself and the growth in both passengers and cargo fell short of expectations.

The White Star and Ryde Lines had entered the route and Compagnie Générale Transatlantique also commenced services to Chile.

Ryde Line had a Belgian Government contract for a four ship service between Antwerp-Montevideo-Buenos Aires-Valparaiso and they put *Leopold II and Santiago* on the route. After a few voyages the service failed. In Chile itself a new coastal organisation Compania Sud Americana de Vapores was founded, based at Valparaiso. To distinguish their ships they chose the red funnel and black top that still exists.

1874 By now matters were serious. White Star and Ryde had withdrawn but their incursion had been minimal. There was simply insufficient business to support a weekly service from Liverpool.

The decision taken by the Court of Directors was to reduce the Atlantic frequencies down to fortnightly in place of weekly.

The steaming time was also lengthened by the introduction of a one knot speed reduction to save coal.

During the year the virtually new *Tacna* was lost by an explosion. *Limena* and *Oroya* (I) was acquired by the Government of Peru.

As part of the need to make the company self sufficient in South America a dry dock had been constructed in Glasgow, dismantled there and shipped to Callao where it was re-assembled. The dock measured 300ft (91.44m) x 75ft (22.86m). Thereafter PSNC's coastal ships were sent to Callao for overhaul.

1875 The effect of the service reduction was to see the laying up in Birkenhead docks of no fewer than eleven of the company's transatlantic fleet. In order to employ the ships the company sought and obtained permission to amend its Royal Charter so as to allow the use of its surplus tonnage on other than the South American route.

Two of the laid up ships went to Royal Mail *Puno* (I) becoming *Para* and *Corcovado* (I) was rechristened *Don.*

1877 Feb: PSNC was approached by Anderson, Anderson & Co, together with F. Green & Co, to see if they would establish jointly with them a steamship mail service to Australia in competition with P & O. The suggested agreement was for a monthly service out via Capetown and homeward through the Suez Canal. A new company was to be formed, the Orient Steam Navigation Company, and was to build its own vessels in the course of time but initially four PSNC ships would be chartered. Orient was to have the option of purchasing the four ships if the service proved to be successful. The PSNC vessels chosen were *Chimborazo, Cuzco* (I), *Garonne* and *Lusitania,* the four sisters built in 1871.

June 28: The PSNC-Orient Line service commenced with the departure of *Lusitania* from Plymouth for Melbourne where she arrived on Aug. 8 (thereby knocking 10 days off the previous record) with a voyage time of 40 days, 6 hours. *Magellan* (I),

Araucania and *Cordillera* commenced the short lived Liverpool-Bordeaux-Buenos Aires service. Losses during the year were *Atacama, Eten* and *Iquiqui*.

1873 The four chartered PSNC vessels on the Australian route proved to be so popular that Anderson, Anderson & Co exercised their option to purchase them (at a later date).

Having established themselves on the route they retained their original names. Furthermore demand was such that a fortnightly service was justified in place of the original monthly sailings.

On the coastal side the Government of Chile purchased *Chile* (II) and *Payta* whilst *Casma* joined the service.

1879 During the year *Mendoza* was delivered for the express coastal service and became the first liner in the world to have electric light. Other new arrivals on the South American coastal routes were *Chala, Arauco, Puchoco* and the second vessel of the *Mendoza* class. Also delivered was *Pizarro* (I). The 30 year old *Bolivia* (I) was taken out to sea and scuttled while the *Illimani* went aground and became a total loss.

Feb 14: Saw the outbreak of the war between Bolivia, Peru and Chile. Peru and Bolivia had signed a defensive alliance in 1873. In 1878 Bolivia imposed an export tax on nitrates. In retaliation Chile occupied the Bolivian nitrate port of Antofagasta and on Apr 5 declared war on Peru. Chile re-purchased the *Amazonas* acquired by PSNC in 1874. The war lasted four years and greatly interrupted PSNC's trade. It also had internal repercussions since the management, especially at local level, tended quite naturally to take sides in the dispute. This was strictly against Head office orders which to this day has always maintained strict neutrality in political matters. It is worth recording that the incumbent Chairman of PSNC is the Honorary Consul for Chile in Liverpool under both present and past Chilean Governments of either party.

Apr: PSNC signed an agreement with their Australia-route partners to operate a fortnightly joint service under the name Orient Steam Navigation Co. PSNC were to add six more ships to the fleet, making ten in all.

May: *John Elder* took the first sailing under the new Orient title. This ship was followed by five more PSNC vessels *Iberia, Aconcagua, Sorata, Liguria* and *Cotopaxi*. The first ship built for the Orient Line, named *Orient,* was the final member of the fleet and made her maiden sailing in November. This ship introduced the "Or" prefix for the mail passenger ships. Both Orient and PSNC used it. PSNC only changed this system of nomenclature when *Reina del Pacifico* was delivered in 1931.

1880 *Callao* (I) and *Pacific* were hulked for coal storage but *Talca* did not have the cubic capacity and was scuttled at sea.

1881 Despite the war there were six additions to the fleet:

Puno (II), *Serena, Arica* (II), *Ecuador* (III), *Osorno* and the tender *Morro* (II). The last two were the company's first twin screw ships. *Peru* (II) was hulked.

During the year the company negotiated a twenty one year extension to its original Charter with the home government. They also introduced refrigeration into their Atlantic steamships so that the carriage of frozen meat could commence.

1882 *Chiloe* was delivered for coastal service whereupon *Santiago* (III) was sold. James G. Robinson succeeded Lawrence R. Bailey as Chairman. *Iberia* acted as a troopship for the Arabi Pasha Egyptian Campaign.

1884 *Cordillera* was lost in the Straits of Magellan whilst *Valdivia* (II) was wrecked at Huacho.

1885 *Manavi* entered service. *Lusitania* and *Britannia* were commandeered for possible use as Armed Merchant cruisers during the 'Russian Scare', occasioned by their invasion, on March 30, of Afghanistan. War was averted when Russia withdrew.

1886 *Oroya* (II) and *Orizaba* were built for the Australian service. These two ships introduced the inbound call at Brindisi, Italy, where the mail was landed for overland rail transfer to London. This saved some six days on the normal Bay of Biscay service. In parallel with this the South American service dropped the mails by tender at

Milford Haven; this saved a day over Liverpool for the London mails. The South American service also carried gold bullion and PSNC owned their own bullion railway vans on the Great Western and London Midland Railways routes.

At this time the Australian service was the life blood of the company. The coastal service being badly affected by the war, and its aftermath, between Chile and Peru. The passenger trade from Liverpool was also still in the doldrums.

1887 *Arequipa* was sold but *Valparaiso* (II) became a casualty.

1888 *Quito* (IV) delivered.

1889 Two more Australian vessels were commissioned; they were *Orotava* and *Oruba* (I), while *Santiago* (IV) and *Arequipa* (II) joined the coastal fleet. *Cotopaxi* (I) was wrecked. *Chimborazo* took the first PSNC cruise to the Northern Capitals.

1890 The ageing *Santa Rosa* was sold for local coastal service use.

1891 The tug *Assistance* entered service.

1892 *John Elder* and *Chiloe* both wrecked.

1893 The changing pattern of the South American trade began to show itself. Cargo carryings were increasing in both directions relative to passenger numbers. As the South American communities grew in prosperity so did their buying power and exports out of Liverpool grew enormously. To cater for this change PSNC ordered their first cargo vessels to supplement the passenger liner fleet.

In reality PSNC were not alone in this; the growth of freight across the world was having parallel effects on the composition of shipping fleets everywhere. Originally cargo was subservient to passengers but by about 1890 this was reversed on almost every world route except possibly Europe-New York. The first cargo vessels to enter the South Amercia trade for PSNC were *Magellan* (II), named to replace *Magellan* (I) broken up a few months earlier, *Inca* (II), *Sarmiento* (I), *Antisana*, *Orellana* and *Orcana* (I). The last two were intended for the Australian routes as was *Orissa*, a passenger vessel.

1894 *Patagonia* wrecked.

1895 William Just, Managing Director from 1843-1875, died aged 83, still serving as a Director.

Chimborazo and *Acongagua* were sold. *Britannia* grounded at Rio de Janeiro and was also sold. *Oropesa* (I), sister to *Orissa* was delivered.

1896 The new delivery was *Chiriqui* for coastal service with *Chile* (II). *Corcovado* (II) and *Sorata* (II) being commissioned, together with the tiny quaintly named *Perlita* (little pearl) for harbour duties.

1897 *Oravia* commissioned.

1898 The Orient Line, due to the economic depression in Australia caused by droughts, was struggling. This resulted in a closer collaboration with PSNC which led to a change of name, the company becoming the Orient Pacific Line. To this concern PSNC allocated its premier steamships. *Galicia* (I) was sold for further service.

1899 At 7,945g the new *Ortona* became PSNC's largest ship to date.

For the Valparaiso-Callao route *Colombia* (II) and *Guatemala* entered service. The lack of any alternative means of transport up the 4,000 mile coastline still ensured that by the luxury PSNC coastal passenger liners was the only way to travel. The weekly mail service still demanded excellent ocean going vessels but the peculiarities of the trade led to a profile that differed from the conventional deep sea transoceanic ships, the main deck was usually open for deck passengers and cattle, the upper deck had staterooms for both overnight and week long journeys; the top-hamper was more box-like simply because the ships were never very far from land and could seek shelter if severe gales were forecast. The one thing that was unthinkable was that they should, as a consequence, be less seaworthy.

Casma, *Osorno* and *Arauco* were sold, each for further trading.

1899-1903 The Boer War. *Orcana* became a hospital ship and *Orissa*, *Orotava*, *Ortona* and *Victoria* became troopships.

1900 *Potosi* (II) was delivered and almost immediately sold to Russia for use in the Russo-Japanese war. *Talca* (II) ran aground at Pochulo Point and became a total loss. *Taboga*, the small coastal steamer, was seized by the Government of Colombia for use as a warship but was released when the Royal Navy intervened.

1901 *Galicia* (II), sister ship of *Potosi* commissioned.

1902 PSNC's Royal Charter was extended for a further 21 years. The crown in the house flag was changed from the Royal Crown to St Edward's Crown. A quartet were built for dual purposes; they were coastal liners but with transatlantic capabilities. *Panama* (III) came first followed by *Victoria*, a tribute to the late Queen, *Mexico* and *California*. Another newcomer was *Gallito* (Little rooster).

1903 *Iberia* was sold and *Liguria* broken up whilst *Arequipa* (II) was lost by being swamped at anchor in Valparaiso roadstead. *Orita* (I) entered the passenger service out of Liverpool.

1904 *Mendoza* was hulked. A number of iron hulled ships were hulked between 1890 and 1904 to replace the older hulks. PSNC still maintained these floating coal and storeships in their major South American ports. It was cheaper and easier to bring the ship alongside to unload and then to tranship via local lighter. At several ports the larger ships did not go alongside a quay but used PSNC pier-like jetties or tenders. On Merseyside PSNC now closed down their 'naval yard' at Birkenhead and dispersed their stores, engineering and maintenance staffs.

The new PSNC berth became Alexandra Dock in Liverpool across the River Mersey.

1905 The big event of 1905 was the sale by PSNC of their Australian route interests to Royal Mail; with it went their share of the Orient Pacific Line plus the vessels *Oroya* (II), *Oruba* (I), *Orotava* and *Ortona*. With this nucleus Royal Mail formed the Orient-Royal Mail Line in February 1906. Yellow funnels were introduced in these ships only.

Orellana and *Orcana* (I) became redundant and were sold to the Hamburg America Line.

Potosi (III) carried on the name in replacement of the 1900 sale of *Potosi* (II). *Ecuador* (III) became a total loss.

1906 Again PSNC demonstrated its propensity to build groups of ships. This time four cargo ships were all commissioned during the year.

They were *Bogota* (II), *Duendes*, *Esmeraldas* and *Flamenco* (I) plus *Ortega* (I), *Oriana* and *Oronsa* for the passenger services. *Callao* (II) was acquired as a replacement vessel but retained for only one year.

1907 *Santiago* (IV) and *Colombia* (II) were lost but seven additional ships were delivered during the period. These were *Huanchaco*, *Junin*, *Kenuta* (I) and *Lima* (III) plus two coastals *Quillota* and *Quilpue* and the old coastal cargo vessel *Explorer* which was part replacement for the losses sustained during the year. *Pizarro* (I) became the last vessel hulked by the company.

1908 *Orcoma* (I) was the company's largest ship at the time of her maiden voyage; she was the first of their vessels to exceed 10,000 tons and was known as the first 'all-electric' ship.

1909 *Lima* (II) was wrecked on the coast of Chile. In May, only three years after Royal Mail had purchased the PSNC's Australian interests, they withdrew from the route. The four ex PSNC vessels were placed within the Royal Mail fleet.

1910 PSNC was acquired by Royal Mail, however, Thomas Rome remained Chairman of PSNC, although the control of the company was now vested in London. Royal Mail's buff funnels replaced PSNC's black livery. One of the other effects of the takeover was a reduction in size of the PSNC fleet, especially on the passenger side. Royal Mail was extremely strong in the Caribbean and with services to Brazilian and Argentinian ports. Both these nations were becoming progressively richer than Chile so that Royal Mail benefited concurrently with the onset of PSNC's less profitable trade. Also underway was the Panama Canal with its threat to PSNC's coastal route.

Already the trans-isthmus railways were siphoning off business to Peru. Furthermore the Argentine-Chile railway was completed in 1910. Numerically, therefore, from the date of the merger the PSNC fleet commenced to shrink. Royal Mail introduced to PSNC its system of issuing debenture stock to raise money for new building. This was repayable out of revenue. The debenture capital came from existing shareholders who received interest income on their investment until it was repaid. The effect was to contain the number of shareholders as well as controlling the group financial policies through a small but immensely powerful group of Directors. The system contained, it may be added, the seeds of later discomfort, mainly because the Court of Directors could raise and use money as they saw fit without having to explain their actions to a large body of risk-money shareholders. *Sarmiento* (I) and *Antisana* were sold and *Lima* (III) was wrecked after only three years of service and *Chiriqui* sank after an explosion.

1912 *Oravia* was wrecked on the Falkland Islands.

1913 *Andes* was built for the account of PSNC, at the owner's wish, but after her maiden voyage to Valparaiso the ship thereafter sailed on Royal Mail routes.
A pension scheme was introduced for PSNC staff.

1914 *Orduna* (I) was launched. After completion she was chartered to Cunard and served on the Liverpool-New York service. It is interesting to note how closely the Cunard design of the late 1920s resembled *Orduna*; clearly Cunard had been completely satisfied with her.
Aug 15: The Panama Canal was opened for shipping. The effect on PSNC was profound. The canal changed the commercial balance of the western Atlantic world. The industrial North East of the United States was now as close to Valparaiso as it was to Rio de Janeiro. From Liverpool the only sensible route to Valparaiso was through the Canal. Chile not Peru became the end of the route. PSNC's investment in building up the Straits of Magellan services were made obsolescent. The Americans, then free from a European war, moved into the commercial opportunities at a time when PSNC were unable to compete. The Panama Canal thus changed trade for PSNC in a manner never to be recaptured. Indeed the far sightedness of the Directors was now demonstrated in full and the joining of PSNC and Royal Mail in 1910 into one group was the company's salvation.

1915 *Orbita* (I) was completed and together with the small *Cauca*. *Orotava* and *Oruba* (I) were transferred from PSNC to the Royal Mail fleet, but *Oropesa* (I) was sold and renamed *Champagne*.
Following the opening of the Panama Canal two ships, *Acajutla* and *Salvador* were purchased from the Salvador Railway Company to operate a feeder service to Panama. *Panama* (III) became a hospital ship.

1916 Feb 2: *Flamenco* (I) was captured and sunk by the German raider *Möewe*.
Nov 10: *Bogota* (II) was torpedoed.

1917 Mar 10: *Esmeraldas*, sister of *Flamenco*, was also sunk by *Möewe*.
Galicia (II) was mined and lost in Teignmouth Bay but *Mexico* was more fortunate; although torpedoed she reached port and eventually re-entered service. In October *California* also became another war casualty.

1918 *Orca* was completed as a cargo carrier and as such was operated by PSNC, but when returned to Harland & Wolff for completion as a passenger ship she emerged in her final format and in Royal Mail colours. *Orca* never served PSNC as a passenger ship.
Apr 28: *Oronsa* was torpedoed off Bardsey Island.
June 25: *Orissa* torpedoed and sunk by U-boat.
July 18: *Magellan* (II) torpedoed.

1919 *Ballena* and *Bogota* (III), two wartime standard ships were taken over as war loss replacements. Three smaller standard type vessels also joined the service. They were *Arana*, *Almagro* (1920) and *Alvarado* (1920).

21

1920 The ex-German *Alda* was allocated to PSNC and became *Magellan* (III). The Admiralty retained *Panama* (III) (renamed *Maine*) as a permanent hospital ship and she therefore did not return to company ownership. *Oropesa* (II) entered the Liverpool-Valparaiso service and *La Paz* was delivered — the first post war custom built PSNC ship. Thomas Rome retired as Chairman to be replaced by Sir Owen Philipps (later Lord Kylsant).

PSNC opened services New York-Valparaiso and New York-Cartagena-Callao. *Ebro* and *Essequibo* came from Royal Mail for the venture and *Quilpue* with *Quillota* acted as their consorts. Against stiff American competition the new enterprise was to be unsuccessful.

1921 *Lobos* and *Losada* joined their sister *La Paz*. With the arrival of these post war ships a gradual disposal plan was instituted. This took into consideration the effect of the Panama Canal on the Straits of Magellan route, plus the reduction of Valparaiso from being first en route port to becoming the terminal.

Corcovado (II) was scrapped. *Orduna* (II), *Orbita* (I) and *Oropesa* (II) were transferred to Royal Mail for a new North Atlantic service.

1922 Jan 4: The ninth extension to the Royal Charter was granted but this time in perpetuity for as long as 'the company shall think fit'. The only proviso that was, therefore, enshrined for the future was the name of the company and its head office at Liverpool. As makeshift replacements for the three liners now on the North Atlantic Royal Mail transferred *Miltiades* and *Marathon* on to the PSNC route and in keeping with tradition they were given the 'Or' names of *Orcana* and *Oruba*. The coastal liners, *Sorata* (II) and *Quilpue* were released and sold for further trading.

Aug 22: At this time Chile passed its 'Cabotaje' law. Cabotage refers to routes wholly within the waters of one nation and therefore outside of International regulations and agreements. It means that advantages can be denied to foreign vessels.

PSNC were extremely badly hit by the passing of this law because in Chile the coastal interport trade was henceforth restricted to ships of their respective nationalities. It is ironic that PSNC was originally founded to provide for Chile, the very service now denied to them. Furthermore the coastal cargo and passenger service had always been a mainstay of their business especially when, over the years, competition from European shipowners had increased and the opening of the Panama Canal had so dramatically changed the emphasis of the trade to Peru and Chile.

1923 *Inca* (II), *Chile* (II), *Peru* (III), *Guatemala*, *Victoria* and *Quillota* were all sold and with their departure PSNC's South American based coastal passenger fleet came to an end. The major PSNC passenger liners, transitting the Panama Canal, acted as replacements. Several of these ex-PSNC vessels had new leases of life under new local ownership and continued on the coastal services.

Laguna was delivered. The other addition during the year, *Lautaro,* came from the Glen Line and was one of the earliest seagoing motorships.

1924 *Oroya* (III) joined the passenger liners while the cargo fleet was augmented by another group of 'L's, all of which were ex-Glen Line motorships. They were *Lagarto, Loreto* and *Loriga*.

To assist in the stabilisation of freight and passenger rates the European, South Pacific and Magellan Conference was reintroduced, following the lapse that the war had brought about.

1925 *Potosi* (III) and *Huanchaco* were sold. These were single deck steamers. The progressive introduction of more loading and unloading ports demanded two or three decks for which the single deckers were not suitable.

1926 *Junin* and *Kenuta* (I) followed their sisters by being sold for further service.

1927 *Ortega* (I) and *Oriana*, now both 21 years old, were sold for breaking up but strangely enough the older *Orita* (I) of 1903 continued in service. In the same year *Duendes* (the only 'D' ever owned by PSNC) went to Greek owners.

1928 Peru emulated Chile by passing its own 'Cabotaje' law.

1929 *Jamaica* was sold after 21 years of Caribbean feeder work.

1930 Yeoward Bros'. *Andorinha* was acquired and renamed *Champerico* to operate the Falkland Islands service from Montevideo.

1931 The company's largest ship thus far was *Reina del Pacifico*, built as an act of faith during the depression. Her speed reduced the round trip time to Valparaiso by 18 days down to 60. To act as consort *Oropesa* (II) was overhauled and her speed increased but she spent much of her time between 1931-1934 laid up. The depression of the early 1930s affected PSNC, who laid up a number of their ships. Efforts to sell some were advocated by the Board. In the midst of all this Lord Kylsant's Royal Mail SP Co's shipping empire foundered and he himself served a term in prison for making false statements in a financial prospectus aimed at raising money. PSNC, owned by Royal Mail, was, by special Act of Parliament, enabled to continue under the control of its creditors, including Martins Bank. A number of the creditors were elected to the Board in order to operate the concern. This state of affairs continued until PSNC was safely out of its predicament.

1932 *Ballena* and *Bogota* (III) were sold as part of the depression slim down. The veteran *Orita* of 1903 went to Morecambe for breaking up.

1933 The ex-German *Magellan* (III), plus *Arana, Almagro* and *Alvarado* all went out of PSNC service and *Orcoma* (I) was broken up at Blyth.

1934 The New York services were finally terminated and *Ebro* and *Essequibo* were both sold for further passenger service. *Ebro* went to Yugoslavia whilst the Russians purchased *Essequibo*. *Champerico* was also sold to Chilean owners.

1936 Civil War in Spain affected the passenger trade to Cuba.

1937 The Falkland Islands Company cancelled their contract with PSNC and commenced to operate their own supply vessels.

1938 *Oroya* (III) was withdrawn after only 14 years service. *Oropesa* (II) was recommissioned to take her place.

Royal Mail once more acquired the shares of PSNC but again kept the two organisations separate by retaining the headquarters of the company at Liverpool. However the Directors of both served on one Board.

1939 Plans to replace the older vessels were promulgated. The fleet by now comprised only 14 vessels. Before the new ships were laid down the Second World War commenced.

1941 Jan 16: *Oropesa* was torpedoed off the coast of Ireland.

1942 May 1: *La Paz* was torpedoed off the coast of Florida. She was sold "as lay" and re-entered service under the U.S. flag. This ship and *Oropesa* were fortunately the only PSNC losses sustained during the war.

1943 Saw the delivery of the first of the 1939 planned replacement ships with *Samanco* and *Sarmiento* (II). PSNC acquired a share in British South American Airways but this investment went when BOAC was formed by the Government.

1946 Two more modified "S" class *Santander* and *Salaverry* were commissioned. The small feeder vessels *Acajutla* and *Salvador* were sold and traded in Greek waters and the transit service through the Panama Canal ceased.

1947 *Salinas* entered service. *Talca* (III) an American Liberty ship managed by PSNC was purchased by them and she released *Lautaro*.

1948 *Salamanca*, last of the "S" class was placed in the South American services. *Lagarto* was broken up after the new arrival's debut.

1950 *Orbita* went for scrap. She and her sister *Orduna*, shortly to follow her, had had magnificent careers with the PSNC and Royal Mail group. Although both had remained on Government service after the war. New ships were *Kenuta* (II) and *Flamenco* (II), purchased on the stocks from the Clan Line.

1951 *Orduna* was finally broken up. *Loreto* and *Loriga* also went to the breakers yard after being out-dated by their replacement tonnage. The new arrival was *Cuzco* (II).

1952 *Lobos, Laguna* and *Losada* were also released by the new arrivals and all three were broken up.

The crown at the centre of the house flag reverted from St. Edwards to the Royal Crown and has remained this way ever since.

1953 The Liberty ship *Talca* (III) was sold to Greek buyers.

1955 New vessels were *Potosi* (IV) and *Pizarro* (II). Two Furness Withy ships were transferred to PSNC management for a two year period; they took the non-PSNC names of *Albemarle* and *Walsingham* and operated a Bermuda-Panama service.

1956 *Samanco* was sold to the German Hansa Line. The *Reina del Mar* was delivered to replace the other *Reina* to give a fleet of 13 ships.

1957 *Sarmiento* followed *Samanco* but into Greek ownership and *Albemarle* with *Walsingham* returned to the Furness Group management.

1958 *Reina del Pacifico* was broken up.

1959 Three smaller cargo motor vessels joined the fleet; they were *Cienfuegos*, *Eleuthera* and *Somer's Isle*. These ships replaced *Albemarle* and *Walsingham* on the Bermuda-Caribbean ports-Panama service.

H. Leslie Bowes became Chairman. In the following year he also assumed the Royal Mail Chairmanship.

1960 The company's first oil tanker was *William Wheelwright*, named after the founder. The ship was an investment project and was placed on long term charter to Shell.

1961 A second tanker *George Peacock*, named after the company's first Captain, was added and BP were her long term charterers.

In Cuba Fidel Castro became President and another area of PSNC trade was denied to them.

1963 Passenger vessels were now no longer a proposition and after a lengthy appraisal of the problem *Reina del Mar* was chartered for cruising to the Travel Savings Association, in which PSNC had a 25% share. PSNC had no wish to continue to employ passenger staff whereas Union Castle had the necessary stewards etc. Union Castle therefore took over the management of the ship and she was eventually purchased by them in 1973.

1965 Furness Withy already had a substantial holding in Royal Mail and now made an offer for the balance of the equity. This was accepted in June and PSNC, together with Royal Mail, became integral parts of the Furness Withy Group.

Cuzco (II) was sold to William Thomson's Ben Line.

1966 *Orcoma*, officially owned by the Nile Steamship Co. joined the fleet. She was a one-off vessel without any sister ships. She introduced the "OR" nomenclature into the all-cargo ships since the prefix *"Reina"* had, since 1931, been used for the passenger liner fleet. With the entry into service of *Orcoma*, *Flamenco* (II) was sold. Already, however, Furness Withy were re-appraising the Group tonnage. They commenced a policy of the inter-group switching of ships and the disposal of older or less efficient ships. PSNC were rife for this treatment mainly because of the heavy competition to the West Coast of South America allied with unsettled commercial and political conditions.

1967 *Sarmiento* (II), *Santander*, *Salavery* and *Salamanca* were disposed of, all for further useful trading.

1968 *Salinas*, last of the "S" class followed her consorts. To replace them three Shaw Savill & Albion motorships came under PSNC management and colours. They were given the traditional names of *Orita* (II), *Oropesa* (II) and *Oroya* (IV).

1969 *George Peacock*, never a successful ship, was sold.

1970 John Gawne became Chairman of PSNC having joined in 1934.

Further inter-company changes took place.

Kenuta (II), *Cotopaxi* (II) and *Pizarro* (II) were transferred, without change of name, to Royal Mail. The three Bermuda ships *Eleuthera*, *Somer's Isle* and *Cienfuegos* were disposed of; the last named going to Royal Mail for a brief period.

1972 *Potosi* (IV), last of the *Kenuta* class, was sold to the same buyers who took *Cotopaxi* (II) from Royal Mail.

1973 After some years in Union Castle colours *Reina del Mar* was finally acquired by them.

The latest additions to the company's fleet were delivered. They were: *Orbita* (II), *Orduna* (II) and *Ortega* (II). Self unloaders their capacity and speed was such that each could replace two or even three of the earlier motorships employed on the route. With chartered Furness Withy extra ships they maintain a three weekly service from South Huskisson Dock, Liverpool.

1976 *William Wheelwright* went aground in Liberia and was deemed to be beyond repair.

Coloso was by now redundant in her role as the PSNC ship based at Antofagasta and was sold.

1978 Two new vessels joined the fleet, *Oroya* and *Oropesa*.

1979 *Orcoma* sold.

1980 The PSNC fleet comprised *Oropesa*, *Oroya*, *Orbita*, *Orduna* and *Ortega*. In the listings in Lloyds Register these vessels are shown as being owned by PSNC subsidiary companies.

Apr: Compania Sud Americana de Vapores acquired *Orbita* and renamed the ship *Andalien* and then *Rubens*. *Ortega* was renamed *Andes* by PSNC and the two ships are operated au-pair with each chartering space from the other to obtain maximum cargo efficiency.

1983 By now the spread of containerisation was reducing conventional fleets with dramatic rapidity. The once numerous P.S.N.C. fleet was now down to three ships: *Oroya* (V), *Oropesa* (IV) and *Andes* (II).

1984 The independent name Pacific Steam Navigation Company disappeared into Furness Withy Shipping. To serve their routage a full container ship (The 'O's carried part loads of TEU's) was delivered. *Andes* (III) joined the seven member Eurosal (Europe South America Line) consortium. Research had shown that the seven faster, larger and specialised (see *Andes* entry) ships could replace the 28 member ships serving the route. The Liverpool headquarters at Wheelwright House was closed and integrated into Furness Withy in Manchester.

1985 In Furness Withy the only remaining signs of the once magnificent P.S.N.C. became the *Oroya* (V) and *Andes* (III) - bearing traditional names.

Sadly yet another great name in British and South American history leaves the scene. It is a sobering and alarming thought that the British Merchant Marine now comprises 920 vessels of which 689 are over 500grt. A mere 3% of world tonnage. In 1900 it was 48%.

Routes

1843-1923	Valparaiso - Coastal ports - Callao.
1846-1923	Valparaiso - Callao - Guayaquil - Panama
1848-1923	Valparaiso - South Chilean ports. The Chiloe service. 9 ports; Terminal Puerto Montt.
1868-19	Liverpool - Bordeaux - Lisbon - Cape Verde - Rio de Janeiro - Montevideo - Punta Arenas - Valparaiso. (From 1870) — Arica - Mollendo - Callao.
1877-1879	Liverpool - Bordeaux - Buenos Aires.
1904-1920	Liverpool - La Pallice - Corunna - Vigo - Lisbon - Recife - Salvador - Rio de Janeiro - Montevideo - Buenos Aires - Port Stanley (Falkland Islands) - Punta Arenas - Coronel - Talcahuano Valparaiso.

1914-1945	Cristobal - Panama Canal - Champerico.	
1920-1930	New York - Panama Canal - Callao - Valparaiso.	
1920-1931	New York - Guayaquil.	
1920-1959	Liverpool - Bermuda - Bahamas - Havana - Jamaica - Panama Canal - South American ports - Valparaiso.	
1920-1937	Montevideo - Port Stanley (Falkland Islands).	
1955-1970	Bermuda - Caribbean Ports - Panama.	
1956-1963	The service of *Reina del Mar* was Liverpool - Pallice - Santander - Corunna (1961 Vigo) - Bermuda - Nassau - Havana - Kingston - La Guaira - Curacao - Cartagena - Panama Canal - La Libertad - Callao - Arica - Antofagasta - Valparaiso.	
1963-	Cargo services operated. Liverpool - Bermuda - Freeport (Bahamas) - Nassau (Bahamas) - Kingston - La Guaira - Cartegena (Colombia) - Cristobal - Buenaventura (Colombia) - Guayaquil (Ecuador) - Callao - Matarani - Arica - Antofagasta - Valparaiso -- San Antonio. "Inducement" ports of call are Manta, La Libertad, Paita (Payta), Pimentel, Eten, Chimbote and Salaverry.	

The Australian services from 1877 are omitted; these are featured in Merchant Fleets in Profile Volume I, Orient Line page 131 onwards.

Livery

Funnel	1840-1909	Black
	1910-1980	Yellow buff.
Hull	1840-1980	Black, green waterline. The waterline colour was introduced about 1870, prior to that no colour was applied to copper sheathing. The early iron hulls were all black.
	1966-80	Red waterline.
	"Reina's"	White hull, green waterline.
Uppers	1840-1868	Brown with some white fitments.
	1868-1980	White.
Masts	1840-1909	Varnished brown.
	1910-1980	"Funnel" buff.
		In 1905 PSNC ships transferred to Royal Mail were given buff funnels.
Lifeboats		The earliest ships had either white or brown lifeboats. There appears to be no set pattern. *Talca* (1862) was the last ship depicted with brown boats. Thereafter lifeboats are white.

Fleet Index

Losada	175	Ortega (II)	217	Rimac	65
Lusitania	56	Ortona	127	Ronachan	95
Magellan (I)	41	Oruba (I)	107	Rupanco	138
Magellan (II)	111	Oruba (II)	182	Salamanca	194
Magellan (III)	171	Osprey	11	Salaverry	196
Manavi	102	Osorno	99	Salinas	195
Mendoza	91	Pacific	30	Salvador	165
Mexico	136	Panama (I)	13	Samanco	192
Morro (I)	22	Panama (II)	33	San Carlos	20
Morro (II)	100	Panama (III)	134	Santa Rosa	63
New Granada	5	Patagonia	42	Santander	197
Oravia	119	Payta	28	Santiago (I)	6
Orbita (I)	162	Perlita	122	Santiago (II)	31
Orbita (II)	215	Perico	133	Santiago (III)	58
Orca	168	Peru (I)	2	Santiago (IV)	108
Orcana (I)	116	Peru (II)	24	Sarmiento	45
Orcana (II)	181	Peru (III)	124	Sarmiento (I)	113
Orcoma (I)	157	Peruano	23	Sarmiento (II)	193
Orcoma (II)	214	Pizarro (I)	92	Serena	94
Orduña (I)	161	Pizarro (II)	202	Somer's Isle	206
Orduña (II)	216	Poderoso	158	Sorata (I)	60
Orellana	115	Portsea	223	Sorata (II)	126
Oriana	147	Potosi (I)	74	Supe	38
Orissa	117	Potosi (II)	131	Taboga	121
Orita (I)	140	Potosi (III)	141	Taboguilla	59
Orita (II)	209	Potosi (IV)	201	Tacna	83
Orizaba	105	Prince of Wales	18	Tacora	68
Ormeda	161	Puchoco	90	Talca (I)	26
Oronsa	148	Puno (I)	62	Talca (II)	130
Oropesa (I)	118	Puno (II)	93	Talca (III)	191
Oropesa (II)	172	Queen of the Ocean	see	Temuco	188
Oropesa (III)	210	1847		Truxillo	67
Oropesa (IV)	219	Quillota	154	Valdivia (I)	12
Orotava	106	Quilpue	155	Valdivia (II)	48
Oroya (I)	81	Quito (I)	8	Valparaiso (I)	15
Oroya (II)	104	Quito (II)	27	Valparaiso (II)	70
Oroya (III)	184	Quito (III)	37	Victoria	135
Oroya (IV)	208	Quito (IV)	103	Walsingham	221
Oroya (V)	218	Reina del Mar	198	William Wheelwright	211
Ortega (I)	146	Reina del Pacifico	190		

Illustrated Fleet List

CHILE (1) PERU (1) BOLIVIA (1)

1 CHILE (I)

B 1840 Curling & Young, Limehouse, London; **T:** 682g.

D 198ft (60.35m) x 29ft (8.84m) x 18ft (5.49m).

E Pad, simple; 2 side lever direct acting 2 x 1 cyl; 2 x 90 HP; Stm P:7 lb; 8 kts; By Miller Ravenhill & Co., London.

H Wood, copper sheathed and guaranteed for 12 years by the builder. Safety boats inverted over paddle boxes; Cargo: 200 tons; Armed with 2 x 2 pounder cannon for protection.

P 116; Crew: 64. When moving under sail alone the funnel was hinged down horizontally and stowed on chocks.

1840 Apr 18: launched; cost £11,935. June 24: maiden voyage, Capt. Glover; Gravesend-Falmouth-Rio de Janeiro-Straits of Magellan-Valparaiso. At Point Famine in the Straits *Chile* and *Peru* (2) met in order that both could steam into Valparaiso at the same time on Oct 16.

1841 *Chile* struck a reef, returned to Valparaiso in sinking condition; repaired. Returned to service with funnel fore of paddle boxes.

1852 Replaced by *Santiago* (6) and sold at Valparaiso; Government owned.

2 PERU (I)

Details as *Chile* (1) except:- **T:**690G.

1840 Apr 21: Launched. July 10: maiden voyage, Capt. George Peacock, Gravesend-Falmouth-Straits of Magellan-Valparaiso. Oct 16: arrived. Oct 25: *Peru* took the first coastal sailing Valparaiso-Callao in a journey time of 8 days.

1852 Stranded and lost. *Peru* was in any case due to be sold after the arrival at Valparaiso of her replacement *Lima* (7).

3 BOLIVIA (I)

Details as *Chile* (1) except:- **B** 1849 Robert Napier, Govan, Glasgow; **T**:773g; **D** 197ft 6in (60.20m) x 26ft (7.92m) x 15ft (4.57m).
1849 Oct 23: maiden voyage, Capt Brown, Liverpool-Madeira-Rio de Janeiro-Valparaiso. Placed on Valparaiso-Antofagasta-Callao route.
1870 Hulked at Valparaiso; used to store coal.
1879 Towed out to sea and scuttled.

ECUADOR

4 ECUADOR (I)

B 1845 Tod & MacGregor, Glasgow; **T**:323g; 271n.
D 120ft 8in (36.78m) x 21ft 6in (6.55m) x 15ft (4.57m).
E pad, simple; 2 cyls; 8 kts. **H** Iron, the company's first **P** 25 plus deck.
1845 Oct: Launched.
1846 Jan: maiden voyage, Capt. N. Glover, Liverpool-Valparaiso-Callao. Placed on coastal service Callao-Guayaquil-Panama. This linked Valparaiso with Panama to connect with the Royal Maid Panama Overland route to Valparaiso.
1850 Found to be too small in service and sold to Pacific Mail SS Corp. of America.
1853 July: Wrecked at Coquimbo.

NEW GRANADA

5 NEW GRANADA (I)

B 1846 Smith and Rodgers, Glasgow: **T**:694g.
D 177ft 5 in (54.08m) x 24ft 7in (7.49m) x 14ft 7in (4.45m).
E Pad, simple; 2 x 1 cyl: Stm P: 12 lb; 8kts; By builder.
H Iron, schooner rigged. No stern galleries.
1846 Aug: maiden voyage, Capt John Williams, Liverpool-Madeira-Rio de Janeiro-Valparaiso-Callao. Placed with *Ecuador* (4) on the Callao-Guayaquil-Panama service.
1851 Disposal not recorded. New Granada was the name of the Republic of Colombia at this date.

SANTIAGO (1), LIMA (1), QUITO (1), BOGOTA (1)

6 SANTIAGO (I)

B 1851 Robert Napier, Govan, Glasgow; **T**:961g.
D 246ft 4in (75.08m) x 28ft 2in (8.58m) x 17ft (5.18m).
E Pad,. simple; 2 direct acting; 2 x 1 cyl; 400 HP; Stm P: 12 lb: 10 kts: by builder.
H Iron, 2 decks. **P** 150.

1851 Delivered Liverpool-Valparaiso, Captain Hind. Cost £140,000 (for 4). This class of four were replacements for *Chile, Peru, Ecuador* and *New Granada.* A glance at the profiles illustrates the advances made in a decade.
1857 Sold to the Government of Peru. Became a frigate. Later a non-seagoing trainingship.

7 LIMA (I)
Details as *Santiago* (6) except:- **T:**1,461g.
D 249ft 6in (76.05m) x 29ft 2in (8.89m) x 17ft 1in (5.21m).
1851 Oct 2: maiden voyage Liverpool-Valparaiso. Averaged 9¾ kts on 2 tons of coal per hour.
1852 Fired on by Guayaquil shore batteries as she called to deliver the mails.
1854 Returned to Liverpool; the company's first vessel to do so. Lengthened and engine compounded. New speed 10½ kts on 1 ton of coal per hour.
1863 July 11: wrecked off Lagartija Island, Southern Chile.

8 QUITO (I)
Details as *Santiago* (6) except:- **B**1852. **T:**1,461g. **D**248ft 8in (75.79m36).
1852 Jan 25: maiden voyage Liverpool-Valparaiso.
1853 Aug: lost on a reef 12 miles from Huasco, en route Panama-Valparaiso.

9 BOGOTA (I)
Details as *Santiago* (6) except:- **B** 1852; **T:**1,461g; **D**248ft 8in (75.79m).
Feb 25: maiden voyage Liverpool-Valparaiso.
1856 Returned to Liverpool for compounding.
1871 Struck a reef off Tarada Point; salved but reduced to a hulk.
1878 Towed out to sea and scuttled.

10 LA PERLITA
B 1853 Bank Quay Foundry Co., Warrington, Lancashire; **T:**140g
D 106ft (32.31m) x 17ft 5in (5.31m) x 8ft 6in (2.59m).
E Pad, simple; 2 cyl; 9 kts. **H** Iron, 1 deck.
1853 Built for Buenaventura (Colombia)-Panama service. June 17: Left Liverpool, Capt Maugham, and disappeared without trace. The journey to Buenaventura was over 11,000 miles, via Straits of Magellan. The delivery voyage was therefore an incredible undertaking.

OSPREY

11 OSPREY
B 1852 Glasgow; **T:**609g.
D 169ft 7in (51.69m) x 18ft 6in (5.64m) x 8ft 9in (2.71m)
E Pad, simple; 2 cyl; 9kts. **H** Iron, 1 deck.

1852 Built as *Osprey* for City of Cork S.S.Co.
1853 Acquired for service Callao-Pisco-Huacho. Lost on the voyage out to Peru.

VALDIVIA, PANAMA (1), INCA (1)

12 VALDIVIA (I)
B 1853 Caird & Co., Cartsdyke, Greenock; **T:**573g;
D 128ft 6in (39.17m) x 21ft 2in (6.45m) x 10ft 4in (3.15m).
E Sgl scr, simple; 2 cyl; 9 kts; By builder. **H** Wood. *The company's first screw steamer and their only such with a wooden hull. Intended as a coastal feeder vessel. In practice these ships were too small.*
1853 Delivery voyage Liverpool-Valparaiso.
1857 Stranded and lost near Valparaiso.

13 PANAMA (I)
Details as *Valdivia* (12) except:- **B** 1854 John Reid & Co., Glasgow; **T:**270g **H** Iron.
1854 Built as a replacement for *La Perlita* (10). Apr: maiden voyage from Liverpool; struck a rock and sank near Point Tamar.

14 INCA (I)
Details as *Valdivia* (12) except:- **B** 1856 Caird & Co., Cartsdyke, Greenock: **T:**290g.
D 130ft 8in (39.83m) x 20ft 9in (6.32m). **E** Compound By Randolph & Elder, Glasgow.
The Invention of the Compound Engine
In 1852 John Elder left Robert Napier to go into partnership with Charles Randolph to form Randolph and Elder.
1853 Jan 24: The partners secured the patent for the compound engine of the vertical direct acting type. The high pressure and low pressure cylinders moved in contrary directions to drive two diametrically opposed cranks. A saving in coal of 30% was achieved. The first vessel to be fitted with such an engine was *Brandon*. These engines are described as compound direct acting.
1856 Mar 15: A patent for a space saving improved inverted type of "V" form was taken out. These engines are described as compound inverted. The first two ships to have this engine installed were *Inca* (14) and *Valparaiso* (15). Only in 1858 did the partners add shipbuilding to their activities by the purchase of the old yard of James Napier and Hoey. In 1868 Charles Randolph retired and the firm became John Elder & Co. In 1885 the company was renamed Fairfield Shipbuilding & Engineering Co. Ltd.
H Iron. 1 deck.
1856 Delivered to Callao.
1857 Placed on Callao-Chala mail service.
1862 by coincidence W. & J. Tyrer & Co., Liverpool introduced an almost identical *Inca* on the South American routes.
1874 Sold; renamed *Union*. Nov: wrecked at Puerto Bueno, Chile.

 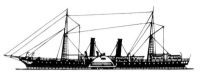

VALPARAISO (1), CALLAO (1), (A) VALPARAISO

15 VALPARAISO (I)
B 1856 Randolph & Elder, Glasgow; **T**:1,060g, 841n.
D 234ft 1in (71.35m) x 29ft 1in (8.86m) x 14ft 5in (4.39m).
E Pad, compound diagonal. 2x2 cyls 320HP; 13 kts. By John Elder & Co.
H Iron. **P** 300.
Note. Drawing 15 is from a painting in the P.S.N.C. Board Room, 15a is from a photograph taken at Puerto Montt in 1870.
1856 Delivered Liverpool-Valparaiso then placed on the Valparaiso-Chiloe service with nine ports of call. Classed, with *Callao* (16) as Express Steamers.
1871 Feb 20: Enroute Calbuco-Ancud, wrecked on Lagartiga Island, Chile.
1976 The wreck, which had been known about locally, was identified and some relics were recovered.

16 CALLAO (I)
Details as *Valparaiso* (15) except:- **B** 1858 John Reid & Co., Glasgow; **T**:700g; **D** 235ft (71.63m) x 29ft (8.84m).
1858 Delivered Liverpool-Valparaiso. For Valparaiso-Pacific ports-Panama service.
1880 Converted to hulk. Based Valparaiso.

CLODA

17 CLODA
B 1857 Glasgow; **T**:699g;
D 214ft 5in (65.35m) x 30ft 5in (9.27m) x 16ft 1in (4.9m).
E Sgl scr, simple; 2 cyl; 9 kts. **H** Iron. 1 deck.
1857 Built as *Cloda* for Irish owners. Recorded as built by Randolph & Elder but at this time all their newbuilding were being compounded by John Elder's yard.
1858 Purchased for South American Pacific Coast services; same name.
1865 Jan 25: Lost off Huacho, Peru, without loss of life.

PRINCE OF WALES

18 PRINCE OF WALES
B 1854 W. Simons & Co., Whiteinch, **T**700g.
D 195ft 5in (59.56m) x 26ft 4in (8.03m) x 17ft 7in (5.36m).
E Sgl scr, simple horizontal direct acting; 2 cyl; 10 kts.
H Iron, **P** 75 berths.

The funnel of the ship had a greater rake than that of the masts.
1854 Built as *Prince of Wales,* red funnel black top.
1858 Acquired by PSNC to replace *Valdivia* (12). Delivered to Valparaiso.
1859 Wrecked on coast of Chile.

19 ANNE
Bt 1854 Chas Rennoldson, South Shields; **T**:344g;
D 153ft 4in (46.74m) x 22ft (6.7m) x 11ft (3.35m).
E Sgl scr, simple; 2 cyl; 9 kts; By Wallsend Slipway & Engineering Co., Wallsend. **H** Iron. 1 dk.
1854 Built as *Anne* for the South American Mining Co., London. Based Valparaiso for trading southwards to Puerto Montt.
1859 Acquired by PSNC; same name; replaced the *Prince of Wales* (18).
1864 Sold, too small.

SAN CARLOS, GUAYAQUIL

20 SAN CARLOS
B 1860 Renfrew; **T**:652g, 444n.
D 199ft 9in (60.88m) x 30ft 2in (9.19m) x 18ft 7in (5.66m).
E Sgl scr, compound; 2 x 2 cyl; 270 HP; 9kts; By Randolph and Elder, Glasgow.
H Iron, brig. **P** 75 berthed.
1860 Delivered for Callao-Guayaquil-Panama service.
1874 Sold.

21 GUAYAQUIL
Details as *San Carlos* (20) except:- **B** 1860 Glasgow; **T**:661g; **D** 208ft 8in (63.60m).
1860 Entered service Callao-Guayaquil-Panama.
1870 Sold locally; used on Callao-Galapagos Island service.
1880 Broken up, Callao.

MORRO (I)   *PERUANO*

22 MORRO (I)
B 1860 Glasgow; **T**:132g
D 119ft 7in (36.45m) x 20ft 1in (6.12m) x 7ft 10in (2.4m)
E Pad. Simple, 2 cyls. **H** Steel; PSNC's first. **P** 120 deck; Crew:16
The drawing is not a positive identification, being taken from a painting the date of which fits Morro's service in Panama.
1860 Built as a passenger tender at Panama.
1881 Replaced by *Morro* (II) (100). Disposal unknown.

23 PERUANO
B 1860 New York; T:639g, 404n
D 181ft 6in (55.32m) x 29ft 6in (8.99m) x 11ft 6in (3.51m)
E Pad; 250 HP. **H** Wood. 1 dk.
1860 Entered service. Based Guayaquil.
18?? Extra accommodation added on boat deck (as drawn)
1874 Sold to Schuber & Co., Guayaquil.
1884 Engine removed and used as a hulk. Appears to have been a warehouse-cum-office.

PERU (II), CHILE (II)

24 PERU (II)
B 1861 John Reid & Co., Glasgow; **T:**1,307g.
D 260ft 5in (79.37m) x 32ft 1in (9.78m) x 22ft 11in (6.98m).
E Pad, compound direct acting; 2 x 2 cyl; 360 HP; 10 kts; By John Elder & Co., Glasgow. **H** Iron, 2 decks.
1862 Jan 1: maiden voyage Liverpool-St. Vincent (West Indies)-Rio de Janeiro-Valparaiso. Then based at Valparaiso. Because of the American Civil War the ship carried three cannon with Royal Navy gun crews.
1881 Hulked. Some records give this ship as wrecked near Layerto in 1863 but she is in Lloyds Register until 1879/80.

25 CHILE (II)
B 1863 Randolph & Elder, Glasgow; **T:**1,672g, 1,174n.
D 274ft 10in (83.77mm) x 36ft 1in (11m) x 22ft 11in (6.98m).
E Pad, compound direct; 2 x 2 cyl; 400 HP; 10 kts; By builder. **H** Iron. 2 dks.
A sister ship to Peru (24) despite the differing details.
1863 Delivered to Valparaiso. Cost £53,650.
1878 Sold to the Government of Chile; same name.
1883 Deleted.

TALCA (I)

26 TALCA (I)
B 1862 Randolph & Elder, Glasgow; **T:**708g, 469n.
D 194ft 1in (59.16m) x 30ft 1in (9.17m) x 16ft (4.88m).
E Pad, compound direct acting; 2 x 2 cyl; 260 HP; 10 kts; By builder.
H Iron, 1 dk and shade dk. First straight stem with a unique profile unlike any other PSNC vessel.
1862 Entered service, Chilean coast.
1865 Under Capt. George Chambers was commandeered by Ecuadorian President

Moreno to put down a local rebellion. *Talca* arrived flying several battle ensigns. When the rebels fled the ship was returned to PSNC and continued her voyage as if nothing had occurred.

1874 Engines removed and used as a storage hulk.

1880 Taken out to sea and scuttled.

QUITO (II), PAYTA

27 QUITO (II)

B 1863 Randolph & Elder, Glasgow; **T:** 1,388g, 1,004n.

D 271ft (82.6m) x 32ft 10in (10m) x 20ft 2in (6.15m).

E Pad, compound; 2 x 2 cyl; 320 HP; Stm P: 25 lb; 13½ kts at 24 r.p.m.; By builder.

H Iron, 1 dk and shade dk. **P** 125.

Designed by Thomas Smith. Cost £48,750. The first of several classes of coastal passenger liners. They carried both cabin and deck passengers as well as deck cargoes including cattle. At most ports of call they berthed stern first. Partly because of the bowsprit but mainly to enable them to leave hastily when the fierce so'westerlies whipped the coast.

1864 Jan 27: maiden voyage Liverpool-Valparaiso.

1865 Sold.

28 PAYTA

Details as *Quito* (27) except:- **B** 1864; **T:**1,344g, 997n.

D 263ft 8in (80.34m) x 38ft 5in (11.71m) x 14ft 11in (4.52m). **E** 400 HP.

1864 Entered service Pacific coast of South America.

1878 Sold to Government of Chile.

29 ECUADOR (II)

B 1864 Glasgow; T: 500g **E** Sgl scr, 100 HP. **H** Iron, 1 deck.

No other details recorded, but disposed of between 1866 and 1873.

PACIFIC, SANTIAGO (II), LIMENA, PANAMA (II)

30 PACIFIC

B 1865 Randolph & Elder, Glasgow; **T:** 1,631g; 1,004n.

D 267ft 5in (81.51m) x 40ft 2in (12.24m) x 17ft 6in (5.33m)

E Pad, compound direct; 2 x 2 cyl; 450 HP; 10 kts; By Builder.

H Iron, 2 dks. **P** 200.

1865 Jan 28: Launched. Apr: Delivery voyage then Pacific coast routes.
1868 This class of four ships was temporarily placed on the Trans-South Atlantic services. They became, as a result, the only compound engined paddle steamers to be used on a transatlantic service.
May 13: Inaugurated the South America-UK direct service. Valparaiso-Sandy Point (Argentina)-Montevideo-Rio de Janeiro-St Vincent-Lisbon-St Nazaire-Liverpool (arrived July 15). There were 170 passengers on the first departure; Captain George Conlan. The cargo of gold and silver was valued at £65,000. The journey time was 43 days.
1880 Hulked.

31 SANTIAGO (II)
Details as *Pacific* (30) except:- **T:** 1,619g.
1865 May 27: Launched.
1865 Sept: Delivered for Pacific coast of South America service.
1869 Jan 13: Left Valparaiso with 172 passengers. Jan 21: Entered the Straits of Magellan. Anchored off Mercy Harbour due to weather. Jan 23: Left and was wrecked on an unchartered rock 2½ miles out. 2 seamen and a child drowned.

32 LIMENA
Details as *Pacific* (30) except:- **T:**1,622g.
1865 Delivered for Pacific coast of South America service. Contract price of £59,000.
1868 Placed on Valparaiso-Liverpool service.
1880 Hulked at Callao.

33 PANAMA (II)
As *Pacific* (30) except: **B** 1866. **T** 1,642g, 1,241n.
1866 Delivered for the Pacific coast service.
1868 Placed temporarily on Valparaiso-Liverpool route. Same routing as *Pacific*.
1869 Replaced by *Magellan* (41) class.
1880 Hulked, South America.

34 FAVORITA
B 1865 New York; **T:** 837g.
D 197ft 1in (60.07m) x 30ft 4in (9.25m) x 16ft 6in (5.03m).
E Pad, single direct acting; 2 x 1 cyl; 200 HP; 9 kts.
H Wood, copper sheathed.
1865 Entered service. PSNC's last wooden vessel.
U.S. riverboat style for calm coastal water work. Very similar to *Peruano* (23).
1871 Feb: Burnt out in Callao Bay.

COLON

35 COLON
B 1861 Randolph & Elder, Glasgow. **T:**1,995.
D 286ft 1in (87.2m) x 39ft (11.89m) x 27ft (8.23m). **E** Sgl scr, compound; 2 cyl; 8 kts.
By builder. **H** Iron, 2 decks.
1861 Built.
1866 Acquired by PSNC to replace the loss of *Cloda* (17).
1872 Sold, Valparaiso.

36 ARICA (I)

B 1867 Randolph & Elder, Glasgow; **T:**740g, 465n.
D 204ft (62.18m) x 30ft (9.14m) x 14ft 7in (4.45m).
E Pad, compound direct; 2 x 2 cyl; 250 HP; 10 kts; By builder. **H** Iron, 1 deck.
1867 South Coast of America service.
1869 Jan 13: Enroute Lambayeque-Callao, stranded off Pacsmayo Point, Peru while entering port. The lighthouse was not lit.

37 QUITO (III)

Details as *Arica* (36) except:- **T:**743g, 468n.
1867 Entered Pacific coast of S. America service.
1882 Hulked. Coal ship at Arica.

SUPE

ATLAS

38 SUPE

B 1867 Randolph & Elder, Glasgow; **T:**298g.
D 145ft 7in (44.37m) x 25ft 1in (7.65m) x 10ft 9in (3.28m).
E Sgl scr, compound inverted; 2 cyl; 50 HP; By builder. **H** Iron, 1 deck.
1866 Sept 29: Ordered.
1867 Entered service. In the PSNC records as 'Pig launch'. Cost £7,500.
1882 Sold, Puerto Montt.

39 ATLAS

B 1867 Paisley; **T:**56g.
D 70ft 2in (21.38m) x 17ft 4in (5.28m) x 7ft 7in (2.38m).
E Sgl scr, simple; 1 cyl; 9 kts. **H** Iron, 1 deck.
1867 Tug at Valparaiso. Towed out by *Supe*.
1890 Run ashore and became derelict.

CALDERA

40 CALDERA

B 1868 Wm. Denny & Bros, Dumbarton. **T:** 1,741g, 1,124n.
D 282.2ft (86m) x 34.3ft (10.46m) x 25ft (7.62m).
E Sgl scr (4 bladed), inverted 2 cyl direct acting surface condensing. 4 athwartship sgl blrs, Stm P 251lb. 440 Hp. 10 Kts. By builder.
H Iron, 2 dks. F: 50ft (15.24m). Cargo: 28,190 cu ft (798.2cu m).
P 99 1st, 39 steerage. Fuel: 600 tons coal.
1868 June 28: Launched as *Assam*, on spec for P. & O who did not buy her. The ship remained with Denny for two years.

1870 Jan 1: Compounded; Denny's first conversion. 2 crank, 4cyl. Stm P 38lb. 11 kts. Jan 4: Struck a dyke in the River Leven. Safely docked.
Aug: Sold to P.S.N.C. for £37,000. She was not successful in service.
1876 Sold to J. Laird, junior. New compound engines installed by Lairds at Birkenhead and lengthened to 335.5ft (102.26m). Emerged with a straight stem. F 66ft (20.12m).
1879 Sold to Compagnie Générale Transatlantique; same name. Placed on Marseilles-New York service.
1883 Overhauled at Le Havre.
1886 Sold to F. Stumore & Co., London.
1887 May: Abandoned at sea off Suakin, Sudan.

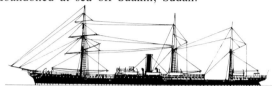

MAGELLAN (I), PATAGONIA, ARAUCANIA, CORDILLERA

41 MAGELLAN (I)
B 1868 Randolph & Elder, Glasgow; **T**:2,856g, 1,791n.
D 359ft 7in (109.6m) x 41ft (12.5m) x 26ft 1in (7.95m).
E Sgl scr, compound inverted; 2 cyl; 500 hp; 13½ kts; By John Elder & Co., Glasgow.
H Iron 3 decks. Cargo: 2,550 tons.
P 145 1st, 75 2nd, 300 3rd.
1868 Dec. 30: Launched. Mar 13: Maiden voyage, Captain C. H. Sivell, Liverpool-Valparaiso to start the monthly advertised service. The 13th being the sailing day — so much for superstition! Cost £74,550 each.
1870 Mar 29: Sailings became twice monthly at a service speed of 12 kts.
1893 Broken up; River Thames.

42 PATAGONIA
Details as *Magellan* (41) except: **B** 1869 John Elder & Co, Glasgow. *(This was the 1869 new name for Randolph and Elder but John Elder died (Sept 17) shortly afterwards.)* **T**:2,866, 1,798n. **D** 353ft(107.59m).
1869 Mar 1: Launched. May 13: Maiden voyage Liverpool-Valparaiso.
1877 March: Transferred to River Plate service.
1880 May 4: Chartered to White Star Line for 1 voyage L'pool-New York.
1890 Tpl exp installed; 3 cyl; 258 NHP; 2 sgl boilers, 6 furnaces; 11 kts; By Naval & Construction Co., Barrow.
1895 Oct 1: Enroute Liverpool-Valparaiso, crew 39, grounded 7 miles north of Tomé, at Lingueral. All saved.

43 ARAUCANIA
Details as *Magellan* (41) except:- **B** 1869 John Elder & Co., Glasgow; **T**:2,877g, 1,807n; **D**: 354ft 8in (108.1m).
1869 Apr 29: Launched. July 13: Maiden voyage to Valparaiso.
1877 July: To River Plate service.
1890 Tpl exp installed as (42)
1897 Sold to Macbeth & Gray, Liverpool.

44 CORDILLERA
Details as *Magellan* (41) except:- **B** 1869 John Elder & Co., Glasgow; **T**:2,860g, 1,791n. **D**:353ft 2in (107.65m).

1869 June 26: Launched. Oct 13: Maiden sailing to Valparaiso.
1877 Aug: To River Plate service.
1882 Sept 20: Lost in the Straits of Magellan.

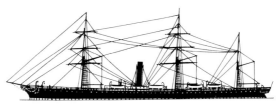

JOHN ELDER

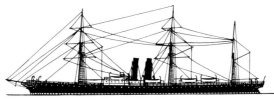

(A) JOHN ELDER

45 **JOHN ELDER**
B 1869 John Elder & Co., Glasgow; **T**: 3,832g, 2,242n
D 381ft 10in (116.38m) x 41ft 7in (12.67m) x 35ft (10.67m)
E Sgl scr, compound inverted; 2 cyl; 550 HP; Stm P: 63 lb; 12½ kts; By builder.
H Iron, 3 dks. 5 steam winches.
P 70 1st, 100 2nd 273 3rd. Crew 104. Fewer passengers than *Magellan*.
1869 Aug 29: Launched; intended name *Sarmiento*. Completed after the death of John Elder. Named as a tribute to the changes affected by his compound engines. Dec 13: Maiden sailing Birkenhead-Valparaiso. P.S.N.C.'s largest ship to-date and the fore-runner of 11 similar vessels. She was well ahead of other passenger ships of the period and compared favourably with the leading transatlantic liners but her 550HP engine was under-powered.
1872 Feb 2: After four round voyages the ship was rebuilt. **D** 406.4ft (123.88m) and new boilering introduced a second funnel (45a). Cost £17,500.
1877 Placed on the joint Orient-PSNC Australian service. Mizzen mast removed. Apr 19: First sailing Adelaide-Suez Canal-Liverpool.
1886 Nov 3: Reverted to Liverpool-Valparaiso route.
1892 Jan 17: Enroute Valparaiso-Talcuhuanco, with 139 passengers, stranded in fog on Cape Carranza Rocks. All saved.

ATACAMA, COQUIMBO, VALDIVIA (II), ETEN

46 **ATACAMA**
B 1870 John Elder & Co., Glasgow; **T**:1,821g, 1,131n.
D 290ft (88.39m) x 38ft 2in (11.63m) x 22ft 9in (6.93m).
E Sgl scr, compound inverted; 2 cyl; 300 HP; 11 kts; By builder. **H** Iron, 2 decks.
1870 Chilean coastal service **1877** Wrecked.

47 COQUIMBO
Details as *Atacama* (46) except:-**B** 1871; **D**:290ft 7in (88.57m).
1869 Dec 7: Launched.
1870 Entered South American coastal service. Cost £42,495.
1901 Hulked.

48 VALDIVIA (II)
Details as *Atacama* (46) except:- **T**:1,162n; **D**:287ft (87.48m).
1870 Placed on South American Pacific coast services
1882 Wrecked off Huacho. 1 lost.

49 ETEN
Details as *Atacama* (46) except:- **B** 1871 Laird Bros, Birkenhead; **T**:1,853g, 1,159n; **D**:292ft (88.7m).
1871 Built for Pacific coast of South America routes.
1877 Wrecked off Ventura Point; 120 drowned; attributed to a change in the currents following an earthquake.

AREQUIPA (I)

50 AREQUIPA (I)
B 1870 John Elder & Co, Glasgow. **T**:1,065g, 662n.
D 231ft 9in (70.64m) x 35ft 2in (10.72m) x 14ft 8in (4.47m).
E Pad, compound; 2 x 2 cyl; 300 HP; 11 kts; By builder.
H Iron. Cargo: 775 tons, Fuel: 180 tons coal.
1870 Jan 26: Ordered as *Casma*. Built for west coast of South America routes. Cost £38,750.
1883 Hulked.
1887 Sold.

HUACHO, IQUIQUE

51 HUACHO
B 1870 Thos. Royden & Sons, Liverpool; **T**:329g, 249n.
D 149ft 5in (45.54m) x 25ft 6in (7.77m) x 11ft 2in (3.4m).
E Sgl scr, compound inverted; 2 cyl; 50 HP; 9 kts; By J. Jack & Co., Liverpool.
H Iron, 1 deck.
1870 June: Built for Peruvian coastal service; Callao-Arica-Iquique route.
1882 Sold at Guayaquil to the Governor of Ecuador.
1894 Owned by M. J. Kelly, Guayaquil.
1914 Deleted from the Register.

52 IQUIQUE
Details as *Huacho* (51) except:- **B** 1871; **T**:323g, 245n.
1871 Feb 12: Built for Peruvian coastal service; based Callao. Cost £9,350.
1877 Wrecked.

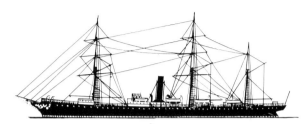

CHIMBORAZO, CUZCO (I), GARONNE, LUSITANIA, ACONGAGUA
53 CHIMBORAZO
B 1871 John Elder & Co., Glasgow; **T**:3,847g, 2,443n.
D 384ft (117.04m) x 41ft 4in (12.6) x 35ft 4in (10.77m).
E Sgl scr, compound inverted; 2 cyl; 550 HP; Stm P: 65 lb; 13 kts; By builder.
H Iron, 3 decks. 5 Steam winches; Cargo: 2,500 tons.
P 80 1st, 100 2nd, 270 3rd.
1871 June 21: Launched. Oct 13: Maiden voyage. Built for the Liverpool-Valparaiso service. The voyage duration to Callao of this class was 56½ days with calls at nine ports. Steaming time was 40½ days at an average speed of 11.4 kts on a daily coal consumption of 47 tons. Cost £91,010.
1877 Chartered to Anderson and Anderson for Orient-Pacific Line service.
1878 Purchased by Orient Steam Navigation Co; same name.
1887 May 12: Final voyage London-Suez-Sydney.
1889 Cruise ship to the Norwegian Fjords.
1894 Sold; renamed *Cleopatra* by P. J. Pitcher, Liverpool. Used for cruising by the Polytechnic Touring Association.
1895 Owned by the Ocean Cruising and Yachting Co., London.
1897 Broken up at Preston, Lancashire.

54 CUZCO (I)
Details as *Chimborazo* (53) except:- **T**:3,898g, 2,439n.
1871 Oct 18: Launched for Liverpool-Valparaiso service.
1872 Jan 13: Maiden sailing. Cost £90,990.
1877 Chartered to Anderson and Anderson for Orient-Pacific Line service. Sept 29: first voyage London-Suez-Sydney. 40 days 12 hours to Adelaide, a record.
1878 Sold to Orient S.N. Co; same name.
1888 Tpl exp fitted; 3 cyl; 615 NHP; Stm P: 150 lb; 3 dbl and 1 sgl ended blrs, 20 furnaces; 15 kts. By builder, now renamed Fairfield S.B.Co. Taller funnel, with fore and aft schooner rig. Derrick gaff on foremast only.
1905 Broken up at Genoa.

55 GARONNE
Details as *Chimborazo* (53) except:- **T**:3,871g, 2,468n; **D** 382ft 1in (116.46m).
1871 Apr: launched. June 29: Maiden voyage on Liverpool-Valparaiso service.
1877 June: Sold for Orient Pacific Line service to Australia via the Cape.
1878 Apr 17: first voyage to Australia for Orient S.N.Co.

1889 July 6: final voyage to Australia then cruising.
1897 Sold to F. Waterhouse, Seattle and used for the Alaska gold rush trade.
1899 Used by U.S. Government as a troopship during the Spanish-American war.
1905 Broken up at Genoa (Bonsor says 1901 wrecked).

56 LUSITANIA

Details as *Chimborazo* (53) except:- **B** 1871 Laird Bros., Birkenhead; **T**:3,825g, 2,494n.
P 84 1st, 100 2nd, 270 3rd.
1871 June: Launched. Sept 29: Maiden voyage to Valparaiso. Cost £91,852. On her maiden voyage a few hours after leaving Valparaiso *Lusitania* shed three of her four propeller blades. No dock was able to take her at Valparaiso and it was not feasible to beach the ship. To enable the spare propeller to be fitted a wooden caisson 24ft (7.31m) x 26ft (7.92m) was built around the stern and pumped dry.
1877 Feb: Chartered to Orient Line, with guaranteed profits, for Australia service. June 28: Sold out of PSNC service and made the first voyage for Orient-Pacific Line Plymouth-Cape of Good Hope-Melbourne in 40 days 6 hours at an average speed of 13 kts. This beat the previous record by 10 days. Her return voyage was via Suez Canal and took 41 days.
1878 Owned by Orient Line.
1886 Tpl exp installed; 3 cyl; 638 NHP; Stm P: 150 lb; 3 dbl and 1 sgl ended boilers, 20 furnaces; 13 kts; By T. Richardson & Sons, Hartlepool.
1900 Mar 31: Acquired by Elder Dempster's Beaver Line (black funnel 2 white bands). Placed on Liverpool-Halifax-St John (New Brunswick) run. July: Reverted to P.S.N.C. for six months.
1901 Feb: Back to Elder Dempster ownership for a charter to the Allan Line. June 26: Wrecked on Cape Race during the charter which was for the summer only.

57 ACONGAGUA

Details as *Chimborazo* (53) except:- **B** 1872; **T**:4,105g, 2,639n.
D 404ft 9in (123.38m) x 41ft 5in (12.63) x 35ft 4in (10.78m). This ship was lengthened by 21ft (6.4m) during construction. Cost £5,685.
E 600 HP; The engine size was increased from 500 NHP during construction; new ones installed. See *Tacora* (68).
P 60 1st, 90 2nd, 335 3rd.
1872 June 6: Launched. Sept 28: Maiden voyage to Valparaiso. Virtually a single funnelled version of the rebuilt *John Elder* (45). Cost £90,970.
1878 Used by Orient-Pacific Line as a stand by vessel.
1880 First sailing to Australia from London via the Cape.
1883 Oct 24: Reverted to Liverpool-Valparaiso service.
1895 Sold to Verdeau et Cie, Bordeaux; renamed *Egypte*. Levant routes.
1896 Scrapped.

SANTIAGO (III)

58 SANTIAGO (III)

B 1871 John Elder & Co., Glasgow; **T**:1,451g, 979n.

D 251ft 7in (76.61m) x 35ft 6in (10.82m) x 22ft 1in (6.73m).**E** Pad, compound, direct acting; 2 cyl: 300 HP; 11 kts; By builder. **H** Iron, 2 dks.
Note: A model aboard the Cutty Sark at Greenwich shows her as single screw but no details of this are known.
1871 Oct 14: Built for the West coast of South America services. £44,000.
1882 Sold.

59 TABOGUILLA

B 1871 Bowdler Chaffer & Co., Liverpool; T:154g, 85n.
D 115ft 4in (35.15m) x 21ft 1in (6.43m) x 7ft 9in (2.4m).
E Sgl scr, compound inverted; 2 cyl; 48 HP; 9 kts; By J. Taylor & Co., Birkenhead.
H Iron.
1871 Based Callao. Tender; single hold.
1893 Out of fleet.

SORATA (I)

60 SORATA (I)

B 1872 John Elder & Co., Glasgow; T:4,014g, 2,573n.
D 401ft 4 in (122.33m) x 42ft 9in (13.03m) x 34ft 1in (10.39m).
E Sgl scr, compound inverted; 2 cyl; 600 HP; 12½ kts; By builder.
H Iron, 3 decks.
P 80 1st, 100 2nd, 275 3rd.
There is a splendid painting of this ship in Callao depicting her paddles and early records give this propulsion. There is no evidence that she was ever intended to be other than propeller driven. PSNC never built paddle steamers for their Liverpool-South America line service; see Panama (30).
1872 Oct 2: Launched, Three months late; was due for launching July 15. Cost £106.725.
Jan 8: maiden voyage; Inaugurated the weekly service Liverpool-Bordeaux-Vigo-Lisbon-Rio de Janeiro-Montevideo-Sandy Point-Valparaiso-Callao.
1879 Transferred to Orient Line management.
1880 Feb 13: first voyage London-Cape Town-Australia.
1886 Apr 29: Last Orient voyage to Australia. Reverted to PSNC service.
Sept 22: Liverpool-Valparaiso service.
1895 Broken up at Tranmere, Cheshire.

CORCOVADO (I), PUNO (I)

61 CORCOVADO (I)

B 1872 Laird Bros., Birkenhead; T:3,805g, 2,406n.

D 387ft 6in (118.11m) x 43ft 1in (13.13m) x 33ft 11in (10.34m).
E Sgl scr, compound inverted; 2 cyl; 600HP; Stm P: 65 lb; 13 kts; By builder.
H Iron. 3 decks. **P** 60 1st, 70 2nd, 240 3rd.
1872 Sept: Built for Liverpool-South America-Valparaiso service.
1873 Feb 19: Maiden sailing.
1875 Purchased by Royal Mail Line; renamed *Don* to replace the lost *Shannon*.
1876 Jan 17: First RMSP sailing; Capt Woolward; Southampton-West Indies. This commander remained with the ship for 18 years and 81 round voyages.
1889 Modernised; T:4,050g, 3,772n; Tpl exp; 3 cyl; 678 NHP; 8 sgl ended boilers, 24 furnaces; 15 kts; By Earle's Co., Hull.
P 245 1st, 26 2nd.
1901 Broken up.

62 PUNO (I)

Details as *Corcovado* (61) except:- **B** 1873; **T**:3,805g, 2,406n.
1873 Built for Liverpool-South America-Valparaiso. May 14: Maiden voyage.
1875 Sold to Royal Mail Line; renamed *Para* to replace the lost *Boyne*.
1876 June: Placed on Southampton-West Indies service. Oct 16: During her second voyage the after hold exploded tearing a large hole in the saloon. 3 killed. The hold had been experimentally converted for carrying bananas in carbon dioxide at low temperatures.
1890 Modernised; T:4,028g, 3,772n; Tpl exp; as (61); By Day, Summers & Co., Northam, Southampton.
1901 Broken up.

SANTA ROSA, COLOMBIA

63 SANTA ROSA

B 1872 Laird Bros., Birkenhead; **T**:1,817g, 1,139n.
D 308ft (93.88m) x 38ft 2in (11.63m) x 20ft 5in (6.22m).
E Sgl scr, compound inverted; 2 cyl; 375 HP; 11 kts; By builder.
H Iron, 2 decks and shade deck. **P** 116.
The deck beneath foremast to bridge deck was open space, not a cabin deck.
1872 Delivered for Valparaiso-Callao-Panama service.
1890 Sold initially to Lota Coal Co; same name. In the same year transferred to Cousino Cia, Valparaiso. Renamed *Luis Cousino*. Operated by Compania Esplotadora de Lota y Coronel.
1902 Broken up.

64 COLOMBIA (I)

Details as *Santa Rosa* (63) except:- **B** 1873; **T**:1,823g, 1,137n.
1873 Placed on Valparaiso-Callao-Panama service.
1890 Sold; broken up.

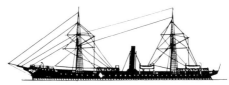

RIMAC, ILO

65 RIMAC

B 1872 Evans & Co., Liverpool; **T:**1,805g, 1,227n.
D 291ft 9in (88.93m) x 40ft (12.19m) x 19ft 7in (5.97m).
E Sgl scr, compound inverted; 2 cyl; 340 HP; Stm P:70 lb; 11 kts; By Fawcett, Preston & Co., Liverpool.
H Iron, 2 decks and awning deck.
1872 Nov: Built for Valparaiso based services.
1877 Sold to Valparaiso Steamship Co., Valparaiso; same name.

66 ILO

B 1872 John Elder & Co., Glasgow; **T:**1,794g, 1,229n.
D 289ft 8in (88.29m) x 38ft 2in (11.63m) x 21ft 1in (6.43m).
E Sgl scr, compound inverted; 2 cyl; 300 HP; 11 kts; By builder.
H Iron, 2 decks.
1872 Jan: Entered service. Cost £47,728.
1882 Hulked.

TRUXILLO

67 TRUXILLO

B 1872 John Elder & Co., Glasgow; **T:**1,449g, 978n.
D 251ft 4in (76.61m) x 35ft 7in (10.85m) x 22ft 4in (6.81m).
E Pad, compound direct; 2 x 2 cyl; 300 HP; 11 kts; By builder.
H Iron, 2 decks. Main deck was open across the breadth of the ship.
P 175 berths.
1871 Nov 14: Launched.
1872 Jan: Entered Pacific coast service. Cost £44,000.
Very similar to *Pacific* (30) class. Built as a replacement for *Santiago* (31) lost in 1869.
1882 Hulked.

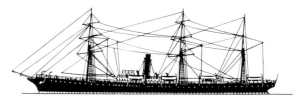

TACORA, GALICIA (I), VALPARAISO (II)

68 TACORA

B 1872 John Elder & Co., Glasgow; **T:**3,525g, 2,279n.

46

D 375ft 7in (114.48m) x 41ft 4in (12.6m) x 33ft (10.06m).
E Sgl scr, compound inverted; 2 cyl; 580 HP; Stm P:65 lb; 13 kts; By builder.
H Iron, 2 decks. **P** 60 1st, 75 2nd, 300 3rd.
1872 May 23: Launched. Reduced in size but with engines built for *Acongagua* (57). Cost £103,475.
Oct 4: *Tacora's* maiden voyage, under Capt. C. M. Stewart, was an attempt to beat White Star Line's *Republic* which was due to sail on Oct 5 Liverpool-Rio de Janeiro-Valparaiso-Callao. Oct 28: *Tacora* came to grief when the vessel was wrecked off Cape Santa Maria near Montevideo. The ship came off the rocks but had to be run ashore to avoid sinking. Three crew and 10 passengers drowned.

69 GALICIA (I)
Appearance as *Tacora* (68) but with details:
B 1873 Robert Napier & Sons, Glasgow; **T:**3,829g, 2,449n.
D 383ft 5in (116.87m) x 43ft (13.11m) x 33ft 7in (10.24m).
E Sgl scr, compound inverted; 2 cyl; 600 HP; Stm P: 65 lb; 13 kts; By builder.
H Iron, 2 decks.
1873 Jan 14: Launched. Apr 23: Maiden voyage to Valparaiso.
1898 Became *Gaspasia,* Canadian Steam Navigation Co., Liverpool.
1900 Broken up at Genoa.

70 VALPARAISO (II)
Appearance as *Tacora* (68) but with details:
B 1873 John Elder & Co., Glasgow; **T:**3,575g, 2,284n.
D 379ft 2in (115.57m) x 41ft 9in (12.73m) x 33ft 2in (10.11m).
E Sgl scr, compound inverted; 2 cyl; 550 HP; Stm P: 66 lb; 12 kts; By builder.
H Iron, 2 dks. **P** 116 1st, 50 2nd, 800 3rd.
1873 July 30: Launched. Oct 8: Entered service Birkenhead-Valparaiso. Cost £129,850
1887 Feb 28: Lost at Vigo, Spain.

BAJA

71 BAJA
B 1872 John Elder & Co., Glasgow; **T:**74g, 8n.
D 81ft 2in (24.74m) x 16ft (4.88m) x 7ft 10in (2.3m).
E Sgl scr, compound; 2 cyl; 35 HP; By builder.
H Iron, 1 deck.
1872 Tug at Callao.

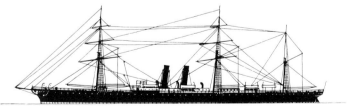

IBERIA, LIGURIA

72 IBERIA
B 1873 John Elder & Co., Glasgow; **T:**4,671g, 2,982n.

D 433ft 6in (132.13m) x 45ft (13.72m) x 35ft 1in (10.69m).
E Sgl scr, compound inverted; 2 cyl: 750 NHP; 4,000 IHP; Stm P: 70 lb; 4 cylindrical boilers, 2 to each funnel; 14 kts; By builder.
H Iron, 2 dks. **P** 100 1st, 150 2nd, 340 3rd.
1873 Dec 6: Launched as the world's largest ship excepting *Great Eastern*. Cost £151,600.
1874 Oct 21: Maiden voyage. Her completion having been delayed by strikes.
1880 May 12: First sailing to Australia for the joint Orient-P.S.N.C. service.
1881 Replaced *Acongagua* (57) as standby vessel on the London-Suez-Melbourne-Sydney route.
1882 Government transport during the Egyptian Arabi Pasha Campaigns.
1883 Jan 25: Placed on regular service to Australia.
1890 June 11: Reverted to the Liverpool-Valparaiso route.
1893 Tpl exp engine; 3 cyl, 600 NHP; 4 cylindrical blrs; 13 kts. By J. Rollo & Sons, Liverpool. At this time yards removed.
1895 *Iberia* made a positioning voyage to Australia to replace a disabled ship. The journey via the Cape was non-stop at 14 kts in 32 days.
1903 Broken up at Genoa.

73 LIGURIA
Details as *Iberia* (72) except:- **B** 1874: **T**:4,666g, 2,980n.
1874 Sept 9: Entered Birkenhead-Valparaiso service. Cost £150,350.
1880 One of four vessels transferred to Orient Line management. May 12: first voyage London-Suez-Melbourne-Sydney.
1890 May 9: Last Australian voyage; Sept 17: reverted to Valparaiso service.
1893 Tpl exp installed; 3 cyl; 600 HP; 15 kts; New boilers; By D. Rollo & Sons, Liverpool; Yards removed from masts.
1903 Sold and broken up at Genoa.

POTOSI

74 POTOSI (I)
B 1873 John Elder & Co., Glasgow; **T**:4,218g, 2,704n.
D 421ft 7in & 128.5m) x 43ft 9in (13.3m) x 35ft 6in (10.82m). This ship was lengthened by 25ft (7.62m) during construction. Cost £10,000.
E Sgl scr, compound inverted; 2 cyl; 600 HP; Stm P:65 lb; 13 kts; By builder.
H Iron, 2 decks. **P** 80 1st, 110 2nd, 350 3rd.
1873 May 14: Launched for Birkenhead-Valparaiso service. Any 6: Maiden voyage.
1880 One of four vessels transferred to Orient Line management. July 7: first voyage to Australia.
1887 May 26: final voyage to Australia; reverted to Valparaiso service.
1897 Broken up at Genoa.

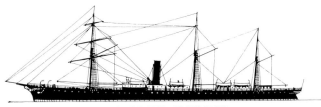

COTOPAXI, ILLIMANI

75 COTOPAXI (I)

B 1873 John Elder & Co., Glasgow; **T:**4,022g, 2,583n.
D 402ft 2in (122.58m) x 42ft 9in (13.03m) x 33ft 9in (10.29m).
E Sgl scr, compound inverted; 2 cyl; 600 HP; Stm P: 65 lb; 13 kts; By builder. The engine differed from *Potosi* (74). A shorter stroke required larger cylinder diameters to achieve the same horse power.
H Iron, 2 decks.
P 100 1st, 140 2nd, 320 3rd.
1873 Mar 15: Launched for Birkenhead-Valparaiso service. June 18: Maiden voyage. Cost £105,750.
1879 Transferred to Orient Line management and placed on Australia run.
1880 Apr 14: final voyage to Australia; reverted to Valparaiso service.
1889 Apr 8: collided in the Straits of Magellan with the German steamer *Olympia*. Beached, careened and repaired there and then.
Apr 15: Refloated but struck another rock and sank. All 202 aboard were saved being rescued by *Setos* of Kosmos Line, Germany.

76 ILLIMANI

Details as *Cotopaxi* except: **T:**2,579g. **D** 402.3ft (122.63m).
1872 Dec 16: Launched. Cost £106,725.
1873 Mar 26: Maiden voyage Birkenhead-Valparaiso.
1879 July 18: Went aground and lost on Mocha Island, coast of Yemen while on the Australian service.

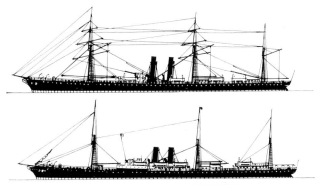

BRITANNIA, (A) BRITANNIA

77 BRITANNIA

B 1873 Laird Bros, Birkenhead; **T:**4,129g, 2,480n.
D 411ft 5in (125.4m) x 32ft 9in (13.13m) x 33ft 9in (10.29m).

E Sgl scr, comp. inverted; 2 cyl, 650 HP; Stm P:65lb.12¾ kts. By builder.
H Iron, 2 dks.
1873 May 27: Launched. Aug 2: Maiden sailing. Cost £140,450.
1885 March 30: Russian troops crossed the Afghan border and were threatened to be faced by British troops. War loomed. *Britannia,* together with 15 other ships, was taken over as an auxiliary cruiser. Apr 22: Taken over at Valparaiso; sent to Coquimbo for conversion. Decommisioned at Coquimbo (the Russians having withdrawn) and sailed for UK to resume service. Rebuilt as (A).
1895 Sept 4: Grounded leaving Rio de Janeiro. Sold locally for £1000. Salvaged and repaired. Sold to Camuyrano y Cia, Buenos Aires.
1900 Acquired by Nogueira, Vives y Cia, Valparaiso.
1901 Broken up at Preston, Lancashire, still as *Britannia.*

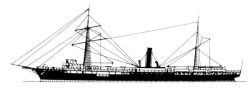

AYACUCHO, LIMA (II), BOLIVIA (II)

78 AYACUCHO
B 1873 T. Wingate & Co., Glasgow: **T:**1,916g, 1,208n.
D 311ft 9in (95.02m) x 38ft 2in (11.63m) x 21ft 1in (6.43m).
E Sgl scr, compound inverted; 2 cyl; 400 HP; Stm P: 65 lb; 12 kts; By builder.
H Iron, 2 decks; **F:**54ft (16.46m).
1873 Coastal services out of Callao.
1890 Hulked.

79 LIMA (II)
Details at *Ayacucho* (78) except:- **B** 1873; *T:*1,804g, 1,132n. **D** 310ft 7in (94.67m).
1873 Built for coastal services out of Callao.
1880 During the war between Peru and Chile *Lima,* commanded by Capt. Steadman, towed a ship full of contraband to Peru. For this he was dismissed.
1909 Lost off the north coast of Chile.

80 BOLIVIA (II)
Details as *Ayacucho* (78) except:- **B** 1874; **T:**1,925g, 1,215n.
1874 Entered coastal service.
1895 Hulked.

OROYA (I), ISLAY

81 OROYA (I)
B 1873 John Elder & Co., Glasgow; **T:**1,577g, 1,117n.

D 270ft 11in (82.58m) x 35ft 6in (10.82m) x 22ft 6in (6.86m). These two ships were lengthened by 15ft (4.57m) during construction. Cost £4,875 each.
E Pad, compound direct acting; 2 cyl; 400HP; 12 kts; By builder.
H Iron, 2 decks.
1873 Jan 27: Delivered for Pacific coastal services. Disposal not recorded.

82 ISLAY

Details as *Oroya* (81) except:-**T**:1,588g, 1,109n. **D** 271ft (82.6m).
1873 Apr 27: Delivered. PSNC's final paddle steamer. Built for Pacific coastal services.
1881 *Islay* carried rifles from Panama to Peru during the Peru-Chile war. The ship was captured by Chilean warships. Although released Captain Petrice was sacked.
1883 Hulked.

83 TACNA

B 1873 Laird Bros., Birkenhead; **T**:612g, 470n.
D 219ft (66.75m) x 26ft (7.92m) x 13ft (3.96m).
E Sgl scr, compound direct acting; 2 cyl; 11 kts; By builder.
H Iron, 1 deck and shelter deck.
1873 Delivered for Pacific local coastal services.
1874 Mar 7: Left Valparaiso for Port de Azucar with a full cargo and on deck 10 cattle and 250 bales of hay. The ship listed sharply in a sudden wind and this was followed by an explosion which blew the deck out sinking *Tacna* with the loss of 19 lives. Her commander, Capt. Hyde, was imprisoned by the Chileans but was released on May 3 after a British protest.

84 AMAZONAS

B 1874 J. Reid & Co., Glasgow; **T**:2,019g, 1,373n.
D 301ft 8in (91.95m) x 38ft 11in (11.86m) x 20ft 5in (6.22m).
E Sgl scr, compound inverted; 2 cyl; 400 HP; Stm P: 65 lb; 11 kts; By Robert Napier.
H Iron, 2 decks and shade deck; F: 45ft (13.72m). P: 18ft (5.49m).
1874 June: Built for Compania Sud Americana de Vapores, Valparaiso.
1877 Acquired by P.S.N.C; same name.
1879 Repurchased by Chilean decree for trooping in Peruvian War.
1881 Having been replaced by P.S.N.C. sold back to Sud Americana.
1886 Not in Lloyds Register.

85 LONTUE

Details as *Amazonas* (84) except: **B** 1873. **T**: 1,648g, 1,121n.
D 299ft (91.14m) x 40ft (12.19m) x 19.7ft (5.97m). **E** By Blackwood & Gordon, Port Glasgow.
1873 Apr: Delivered to Cia. Sud Americana de Vapores, Valparaiso.
1877 Acquired by P.S.N.C; same name.
1879 Chartered to the Chilean Government as coastal supply vessel. It was stipulated

in the contract that she was not to be used in the war.
1881 Replaced by P.S.N.C. and therefore resold to Sud Americana.
1888 Ownership reverted to P.S.N.C. but Chilean flag. Converted into a hulk at some unrecorded date.

LOBO

86 LOBO
1874 John Elder & Co., Glasgow. T:106g.
D 89ft 7in (27.3m) x 18ft 4in (5.59m) x 8ft 9in (2.66m).
E Sgl scr, compound, 27 cyl **H** Iron
1874 Feb: Water launch at Callao. Cost £4,950. No other details.

CASMA (II), CHALA

87 CASMA (II)
B 1878 Laird Bros., Birkenhead; **T:**592g, 358n.
D 180ft 5in (54.99m) x 30ft 1in (9.17m) x 14ft 9in (4.50m).
E Sgl scr, compound inverted; 2 cyl; 95 HP; 10 kts; By builder.
H Steel, 2 decks; 3 masts; quarter deck 46ft (14.02m). **P** 40.
1878 Nov: The company's first steel hull. Coastal services.
1899 Sold to J. J. McAuliffe & Co, Valparaiso; based Coquimbo. Same name.
1900 Sold to Government of Costa Rica.
1910 Dismantled.

88 CHALA
Details as *Casma* (87) except: **T:**598g, 358n.
1878 West coast coastal service vessel.
1897 Hulked

ARAUCO, PUCHOCO

89 ARAUCO
B 1879 Gourlay Bros., Dundee; **T:**801g, 672n.
D 200ft (60.96m) x 29ft 2in (8.89m) x 15ft 6in (4.72m).
E Sgl scr, compound; 2 cyl; 105 HP; 10 kts; By builder.
H Iron, 3 decks; F: 20ft (6.1m); P: 60ft (18.29m).
1879 Apr: Built for South American services.
1899 Sold to J. J. McAulliffe & Co., Valparaiso. Recorded as *Almirante Latorre* but Lloyds lists her as *Arauco* until 1909. Registered at Coquimbo, Chile.
1909 Out of service.

90 PUCHOCO
Details as *Arauco* (89) except:- **T**:804g, 673n.
1879 Entered service.
1899 Sold; renamed *Isidora*, J. J. McAuliffe & Co., Valparaiso.
1900 Transferred to Cia Esplotadora de Lota y Coronel, Valparaiso.
1906 Wrecked.

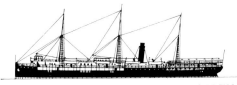

MENDOZA, PIZARRO, PUNO (II), SERENA

91 MENDOZA
B 1879 Robert Napier & Sons, Glasgow; **T**:2,160g, 1,357n.
D 320ft (97.54m) x 40ft 4in (12.29m) x 20ft 8in (6.3m).
E Sgl scr, compound inverted; 2 cyl; 300 HP; 11 kts; By builder.
H Steel, 2 decks; F: 40ft (12.19m); 3 masts. **P** 100 1st.
The first British ship to use electricity from a Gramme generator although the first experiments were in HMS Minotaur.
1879 South American coastal passenger service Valparaiso-Callao.
1904 Hulked.

92 PIZARRO
Details as *Mendoza* (91).
1879 Entered coastal passenger service.
1907 Hulked.

93 PUNO (II)
Details as *Mendoza* (91) except: **B**: 1881; **T**:2,398g, 1,504n.
1881 Entered coastal passenger service.
1904 Hulked.

94 SERENA
Details as *Mendoza* (91) except: **B** 1881; **T**:2,394g, 1,502n.
1881 Entered coastal passenger service.
1903 Hulked.

95 RONACHAN
T:1,156g.
Formerly a sailing vessel.
1881 PSNC opened up a connection to Diego Garcia and this hulk was purchased from Rankin Gilmour for stationing there. Over the years PSNC had acquired a number of coal storage hulks and located them at refuelling points. Very few of these ex-sailing ships are recorded because they appear in no sailing lists.

96 **ARRAN**

T:962g. Formerly a sailing vessel.
1881 Purchased with *Ronachan* (95) for stationing at Diego Garcia.

ARICA (II), ECUADOR (III)

97 **ARICA (II)**

B 1881 Laird Bros., Birkenhead; **T:**1,771g, 1,310n.
D 300ft (91.44m) x 36ft 2in (11.02m) x 19ft 4in (5.89m).
E Sgl scr, compound inverted; 2 cyl; 220 HP; 11 kts; By builder.
H Steel, 2 decks; F: 40ft (12.19m).
1881 Coastal services.
189? Hulked.

98 **ECUADOR (II)**

Details as *Arica* (97) except:- **T:**1,768g, 1,310n.
1881 Entered service, Pacific coastal routes.
1916 July 4: foundered 14 miles off Constitucion, Chile.

OSORNO

99 **OSORNO**

B 1881 Scott & Co., Greenock; **T:**532g, 308n.
D 176ft 2in (53.69m) x 27ft 1in (8.25m) x 13ft 9in (4.19m).
E Tw scr, compound; 2 x 2 cyl; 90 HP; 11 kts; By builder.
H Steel, 1 dk. Open topped bridge.
1881 Oct: Entered service Valparaiso-South Chilean ports.
1899 Nov: Sold to the Government of Nicaragua. Armed transport.

MORRO (II)

100 **MORRO (II)**

B 1881 Scott & Co., Greenock; **T:**170g, 69n.
D 125ft 9in (28.30m) x 23ft (7.01m) x 8ft (2.44m).
E Tw scr, comp; 2 x 2 cyl; 90 HP; 11 kts. By builder.
H Steel. 1dk, schooner rigged.
1881 Aug: Replaced the first *Morro* (22) as the Panama tender.
1902 Sold to J. J. McAuliffe, Valparaiso as *Morro*.
1906 Renamed *Araucancita*; as drawn.
1909 Became *Aramac*; same owner.

1911 Sold to Sociedad Lobitos Oilfield Ltda, Callao. Same name. This company was a C. T. Bowring subsidiary.
1922 Broken up.

CHILOE

101 CHILOE

B 1882 John Elder & Co., Glasgow; **T:** 2,309g, 1,326n.
D 321ft (97.84m) x 37ft 4in (11.38m) x 24ft 9in (7.54m).
E Sgl scr, compound inverted; 2 cyl; 400 HP; 11 kts; By builder.
H Iron, 2 decks. The last iron hulled vessel built for PSNC.
1882 Entered Pacific coast service.
1892 July: Lost at Talcahuano en route Valparaiso — Puerto Montt.

MANAVI, QUITO (IV)

102 MANAVI

B 1885 Robert Napier & Sons, Glasgow: **T:**1,041g, 615n.
D 216ft (65.84m) x 35ft 1in (10.69m) x 15ft (4.57m).
E Sgl scr, compound; 2 cyl; 90 HP; 10 kts; By builder.
H Steel, 2 decks and shade deck. P 54.
1885 May: Built for Pacific coast services.
1890 New boilers.
1920 Sold; out of service, presumed scrapped being 35 years old — but see *Quito* (103)!

103 QUITO (IV)

Details as *Manavi* (102) except:- **B** 1888 Laird Bros., Birkenhead; **T:**1,089g, 815n.
E Tpl exp; 3 cyl: 93 RHP; 10 kts; By builder.
1888 Entered service.
1915 According to PSNC records sold to Royal Mail Line but not listed as owned by them. Lloyds Register gives the owner as Etchegaray Onfray & Co., Valparaiso.
1925 Broken up.

OROYA (II), ORIZABA

104 OROYA (II)

B 1886 Barrow Shipbuilding Co., Barrow; **T:** 6,057g, 3,359n.

D 474ft (144.47m) oa, 460ft (140.21m) x 49ft 4in (15.03m) x 35ft 4in (10.77m).
E Sgl scr, tpl exp; 3 cyl. 1,200 HP, 7,000 IHP; 12½ kts; By Naval Construction & Armament Co., Barrow.
H Steel, 4 decks and dbl bottom; F: 47ft (14.32m), P: 35ft (10.66m).
P 126 1st, 154 2nd, 412 3rd (in two tiered bunks).
PSNC's first straight stemmed ocean liner and the largest vessel yet built for the company.
1886 Aug 31: Launched. Designed for the Australian service
1887 Feb 17: Maiden voyage London-Suez Canal-Melbourne-Sydney.
1895 Mar 4: Went aground and was severely damaged in the Bay of Naples.
1905 Refitted during which the funnels were heightened.
1906 Feb: Sold to Royal Mail Line for Orient-Royal Mail Line service.
1909 Broken up in Italy; renamed *Oro* for the delivery voyage.

105 ORIZABA

Details as *Oroya* (104) except:- **T**:6,077g.
1886 Built for PSNC but placed on the Orient Line managed Australian route via Suez Canal.
Sept 30: maiden voyage Southampton-Suez-Melbourne-Sydney.
1905 Feb 17: ran aground and wrecked in a dense smoke haze set up by bush fires off Garden Island, Sydney, Australia. The wreck was finally sold for £3,750.

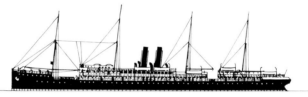

OROTAVA, ORUBA (I)

106 OROTAVA

B 1889 Barrow Shipbuilding Co., Barrow; **T**:5,857g, 3,096n.
D 430ft (131.06m) x 49ft 3in (15.03m) x 34ft 2in (10.42m).
E Sgl scr, tpl exp; 3 cyl. 1,030 HP, 7,000 IHP; Stm P: 60 lb; 14½ kts; By Naval Construction & Armament Co., Barrow.
H Steel, 2 decks; F: 66ft (20.1m), P: 48ft (14.63m).
P 126 1st, 120 2nd, 400 3rd.
1889 Built for Liverpool-Valparaiso service; made two voyages before being transferred to Orient Line management and the Australian service via Suez.
1890 June 6: First voyage London-Suez-Melbourne-Sydney.
1896 Capsized whilst coaling at Tilbury; 4 lost. Raised and renovated.
1897 Resumed service to Australia.
1899-1903 Boer War transport *No 91*. Retained, as did the majority, her P.S.N.C. colours.
1903 Mar 13: returned to Australian route.
1906 Feb: ownership passed to Royal Mail Line. Yellow funnels. Remained on Australian berth.
1909 Mar 5: Last voyage to Australia; transferred to West Indies services. Pass: 250.
1914 Joined "B" Line of 10th Cruiser Squadron.
1919 Sold and broken up.

107 **ORUBA (I)**

Details as *Orotava* (106) except:- **T**:5,852g, 3,351n.
1889 Built for Liverpool-Valparaiso service.
1890 Transferred to Orient Line service.
July 4: First sailing to Australia.
1906 Feb: Transferred to Royal Mail Line ownership, given yellow funnels; remained on Australian route.
1908 Oct 16: final sailing to Australia; placed on Royal Mail's South American service to Buenos Aires.
1914 Purchased by the British Admiralty and rebuilt to represent the battleship HMS *Orion*.
1915 Scuttled at Mudros Harbour, Aegean Sea, as a breakwater.

SANTIAGO (IV), AREQUIPA (II)

108 **SANTIAGO (IV)**

B 1889 Barrow Shipbuilding Co., Barrow; **T**:2,953g, 1,366n.
D 350ft (106.68m) x 45ft 2in (13.77m) x 22ft 6in (6.86m).
E Sgl scr, tpl exp; 3 cyl: 31in (78.74cm), 49in (124.46cm) and 76in (193.04cm); Stroke: 60in (152.4cm); 471 NHP; 12 kts; By Naval Armaments & Construction Co., Barrow.
H Steel, 2 decks; F: 72ft (21.95m), P: 28ft (8.53m).
P 130
1889 Entered coastal passenger service Valparaisco-Callao.
1907 June 18: lost near Corral.

109 **AREQUIPA (II)**

Details as *Santiago* (108) except:- **T**:2,953g, 1,387n.
1889 Delivered for coastal passenger service Valparaiso-Callao.
1903 June 2: caught by a sudden 'Northerner' gale at Valparaiso buoys during the handling of her cargo.
The crew and shore staff fought to hold the ship but, during an intensely violent series of gusts, the ship suddenly keeled over and sank. Of the 100 aboard over 80 lives were lost.

ASSISTANCE

110 **ASSISTANCE**

B 1891 Gourlay Bros & Co., Dundee; **T**:214g, 60n.
D 105ft (32m) x 22ft 7in (6.88m) x 12ft (3.66m).
E Sgl scr, compound; 2 cyl: 17in (43.18cm) and 34in (86.36cm); Stroke: 24in (60.96cm); 63 RHP; By builder.
H Steel, 1 deck.
1891 Tug; initially based at Liverpool but later in Chile.
1926 Sold to Oelckers Hermanos, Chile. Renamed *Tautil*.
1929 July: Wrecked near Lota.

MAGELLAN (II), INCA (II), SARMIENTO (I), ANTISANA

111 MAGELLAN (II)
B 1893 Harland & Wolff, Belfast; **T**:3,590g, 2,320n. 5,032 dwt.
D 360ft 7in (109.91m) x 43ft 2in (13.16m) x 27ft 1in (8.25m).
E Sgl scr, tpl exp; 3 cyl. 302 NHP; 2,100 IHP; 12 kts; By builder.
H Steel, 2 decks; F:42ft (12.8m), B:96ft (29.26m), P:40ft (12.19m); Cargo: 234,000 cu ft (6.622 cu m) in 4 holds served by 9 derricks. Crew:40. Coal: 1235 tons at 35.2 per day.
1893 Cargo vessels UK-West Coast of South America services. Carried 12 2nd class passengers. The wheelhouse was in the poop.
1918 July 25: Torpedoed and sunk 53 miles N.E. of Cape Serrat. 1 lost.

112 INCA (II)
Details as *Magellan* (111) except:- **T**:3,593g, 2,322n.
1893 Entered general cargo services to South America.
1923 Sold; renamed *Llanquihue* Soc. Anon. y Comercial Braun y Blanchard, Punta Arenas, Argentine.
1929 Broken up.

113 SARMIENTO (I)
Details as *Magellan* (111) except:- **T**:3,603g, 2,332n.
D 361ft (110.03m).
1893 Cargo vessel.
1910 Sold to Messageries Maritimes, Marseilles; renamed *Normand*. Used to establish a UK-French channel ports - Black Sea service for the French Government.
1923 Broken up in Italy.

114 ANTISANA
Details as *Magellan* (111) except:- **T**:3,584g, 2,317n.
1893 Built for South American cargo services.
1910 Became *Basque* of Messageries Maritimes for same service as *Normand*.
1918 Feb 18: Torpedoed by *UB 52*, 1100 hrs, at Marsa Sirocco. Second Engineer Achille Vidal fought a fire on board until burnt to death. He was awarded the Legion d'Honneur. Feb 20: Beached at Malta.
1920 Dec: Resumed her pre-war service to the Black Sea.
1923 Nov: Broken up in Italy.

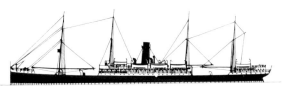

ORELLANA, ORCANA (I)

115 ORELLANA

Bt 1893 Harland & Wolff, Belfast; **T**:4,821g, 3,095n.
D 401ft (122.22m) x 47ft 7in (14.5m) x 19ft 11in (6.07m).
E Sgl scr, tpl exp; 3 cyl. 483 NHP; 11 kts; By builder.
H Steel, 3 dks; **F** 41ft (12.5m) **B** 147ft (44.8m) **P** 57ft (17.37m).
P 70 1st, 675 Emigrants.
1892 Dec 7: Launched.
1893 Apr 12: Maiden voyage; cargo services being her main role the emigrants being carried from Spain and Portugal seasonally.
1904 Sold to Hamburg America Line; renamed *Allemania*.
1906 Sold to Russian Government; renamed *Kowno*. She replaced vessels lost in the Russo-Japanese war which had now ended.
1907 Reverted to Hamburg America ownership and *Allemania*.
1917 Apr: Seized by the USA: renamed *Owasco* and operated by the United States Shipping Board.
1917 Dec 10: Torpedoed by a German submarine off Alicante. Beached but beyond commercial repair.
1918 Broken up in Spain.

116 ORCANA (I)

Details as *Orellana* (115) except: **T**:4,803g, 3,080n.
1893 March 7: Launched. July 19: Maiden sailing. Same duties as her sister.
1899-1903: Boer War hospital ship. Became Transport *No 40*, yellow funnel and white hull.
1904 Sold to Hamburg America Line, renamed *Albingia*.
1906 Transferred to Russian Government for collier duties; renamed *Grodno*. Because the war was over (Treaty of Portsmouth, USA, Aug 29 1905) she reverted in 1907 to *Albingia*.
1917 Apr: Seized by US Government; renamed *Argonaut*, War Shipping Board.
1918 June 5: Sunk by *U-82* off Bishop Rock.

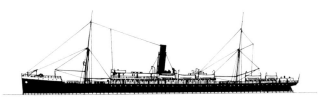

ORISSA, OROPESA (I), ORAVIA

117 ORISSA

B 1895 Harland & Wolff, Belfast; **T**:5,317g, 3,320n.
D 421ft (128.32m) x 48ft 9in (14.86m) x 33ft (10.06m).
E Tw scr, tpl exp; 2 x 3 cyl. 568 NHP; 15 kts; 2 dbl ended blrs. By builder. Coal: 1586 tons at 84 tons per day.

H Steel, 3 dks. F:64ft (19.51m). **P** 70 1st, 104 2nd, 456 3rd. Crew: 120.
1894 Dec 15: Launched.
1895 Apr 11: Maiden voyage to Valparaiso.
1899-1904 Boer War Transport *No 18*. Brought home Lord Kitchener, Sir John French and Sir Ian Hamilton from Cape Town at the end of the war. During this period had deck houses between fcsle and fore-mast plus two pairs of vents the aftermost to bridge height.
1906 Aug: Was berthed at Valparaiso during the earthquake and used as a refugee accommodation ship.
1918 June 25: Torpedoed and sunk 21 miles southwest of Skerryvore, 6 dead.

118 OROPESA (I)
Details as *Orissa* (117) except:- **T**:5,303g, 3,308n.
1894 Nov 29: Launched.
1895 Feb 28: Maiden voyage to Valparaiso; Captain Hayes.
1914 Nov: Became an Armed Merchant Cruiser of the 10th Cruiser Squadron. 6 x 6in (15.24cm) and 2 x 6 pounders. Captain Percy Brown.
1915 Mar: Sank a U-boat off Skerryvore, Scotland. Dec: Transferred to the French Navy; renamed *Champagne* but retained her British crew.
1917 Oct 15: Torpedoed in the Irish Sea and sunk. 56 lost.

119 ORAVIA
Details as *Orissa* (117) except: **B** 1897. **T**:5,321g, 3,318n.
1896 Dec 5: Launched.
1897 July 1: Maiden voyage to Valparaiso.
1912 Nov 12: During one of the occasional calls at the Falklands went aground on Billy Rock, Seal Rocks, Port Stanley, Liverpool-Callao. Nov 16: Abandoned.

CHIRIQUI, TABOGA

120 CHIRIQUI
B1896 Wigham Richardson & Co., Newcastle; **T**:643g, 343n.
D 185ft (56.39m) x 31ft 1in (9.47m) x 12ft 9in (3.89m).
E Sgl scr, compound inverted; 2 cyl; 90RHP; 11 kts; By builder.
H Steel, 1 deck; F:22ft (6.7m), shade deck 164ft (49.99m). The fcsle, as in the drawing, has the appearance of being a half deck and no poop measurement is listed.
1896 Built for coastal services.
1910 Sunk by explosion.

121 TABOGA
Details as *Chiriqui* (120) except:- **T**:649g, 348n.
1898 Built for coastal services.

1901 Seized for war purposes by the Government of Colombia; a British gun-boat retrieved the situation.
1909 Sold to Pinel Bros., Panama; same name.
1911 May: wrecked.

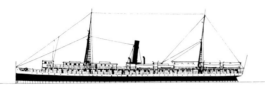

PERLITA

122 **PERLITA**
B 1896 Laird Bros., Birkenhead; **T**:49g, 8n.
D 62ft (18.9m) x 15ft 4in (4.67m) x 6ft 2in (1.9m).
E Sgl scr, compound; 2 cyl. **H** Steel, 1 deck.
1896 Steam launch for service to PSNC vessel lying at the buoys in Valparaiso roadstead. This vessel had permanent wooden awnings over the stern and midship house. The funnel may have been brass not black.

CHILE (III), PERU (III)

123 **CHILE (III)**
B 1896 Caird & Co., Greenock; **T**:3,225g, 1,702n.
D 350ft 4in (106.78m) x 43ft 1in (13.13m) x 19ft 5in (5.92m).
E Tw scr, tpl exp; 2 x 3 cyl; 324 NHP; 12½ kts; By builder.
H Steel, 2 decks and shade deck. **P** 100 1st, 50 2nd, 300 3rd (deck).
1896 Built for Valparaiso-Callao route.
1921 Transferred to Valparaiso-Cristobal service.
1923 Sold; renamed *Flora*, Soc. Maritima y Comercial R. W. James y Cia, Valparaiso.
1934 Broken up.

124 **PERU (III)**
Details as *Chile* (123) except:- **T**:3,225g, 1,702n.
1896 Built for Valparaiso-Callao route.
1921 Transferred to Valparaiso-Cristobal service.
1923 Sold to Soc. Anon. Gonzalez Soffia y Cia as *Peru*. A white "S" being added to the funnel.
1928 Sold to Soc. Anon. Maritima Chilena; same name.
1944 Broken up.

CORCOVADO (II), SORATA (II)

125 **CORCOVADO (II)**
B 1896 C. S. Swan & Hunter, Newcastle: **T**:4,568g, 2,950n.
D 390ft (118.87m) x 47ft 2in (14.38m) x 30ft (9.14m).

E Sgl scr, tpl exp, 3 cyl, 2,300 IHP, 311 NHP, 10¾ kts. By Wallsend Slipway Co, Newcastle.
H Steel, 3 dks. F:52ft (15.86m). Cargo 312,000 cu ft (8,830 cu m). Fuel 943 tons coal at 36 tons per day. **P** 12 2nd. Crew 51.
1896 Cargo services UK ports to most West coast South American ports.
These ships had the wheelhouse in the poop.
1921 Broken up.

126 **SORATA (II)**
Details as *Corcovado* (125) except:- **B** 1897; **T**:4,581g, 2,943n.
1897 Entered service.
1914-18 Government service.
1922 Sold; renamed *Otto Fischer* by Schroder, Holken und Fischer, Hamburg. Used as a cargo vessel only. In the same year this company acquired the coaster *Westerbroek* and also renamed this ship *Otto Fischer*. This ship remained in service until 1934. The assumption is that the *Sorata* was disposed of in late 1922 and was broken up.

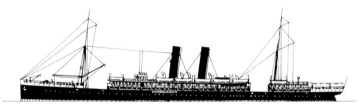

ORTONA

127 **ORTONA**
B 1899 Vickers, Sons and Maxim, Barrow; **T**:7,945g, 4,115n.
D 515ft (156.97m) oa, 500ft (152.4m) x 55ft 4in (16.88m) x 33ft 7in (10.27m).
E Tw scr, tpl exp; 2 x 3 cyl; 560 HP; Stm P: 190lb; 4 dbl ended boilers, 16 furnaces; 14 kts; By Naval Construction & Armament Co., Barrow (i.e. Builder).
H Steel, 2 decks; F:66ft (20.1m).
P 130 1st, 162 2nd, 300 3rd (steerage class).
1899 Nov 24: maiden voyage to Australia under the joint Orient-PSNC service. No sisters; not even near relatives were built.
1902 June: Trooping duties to South Africa, as Transport number 12.
1903 Oct 9: Returned to the Australian route.
1906 Feb: Acquired by Royal Mail together with remainder of PSNC fleet.
1909 Apr 30: Last Australian voyage.
1910 Renamed *Arcadian* and converted into a cruise ship. Pass 320 one class.
1915 Troopship. Gallipoli Headquarters ship to Sir Ian Hamilton.
1917 Apr 15: Torpedoed in Eastern Mediterranean en-route Salonika-Alexandria. 279 lives lost, out of 1,335 aboard.

COLOMBIA (II)

128 **COLOMBIA (II)**
B 1899 Caird & Co., Greenock; **T**:3,335g, 1,764n.

D 359ft 4in (109.52m) x 43ft 2in (13.16m) x 19ft 4in (5.89m).
E Tw scr, tpl exp; 2 x 3 cyl; 324 HP; 12½ kts; By builder.
H Steel, 2 decks and shade deck. **P** 1st, 2nd and 3rd carried.
1899 Built for Pacific coast express service. Her engines were identical to those installed in *Chile* (123) and *Peru* (124) in 1896.
1907 Aug 9: Lost off Lobos de Tierra, Peru.

GUATEMALA

129 GUATEMALA

Details as *Colombia* (128) except:- **B** 1899 Caird & Co, Greenock; **T:**3,227g, 1,757n. **D** 359 .3ft (109.52m). The hulls and engines of these two ships were the same. But they were not sisters in appearance. The reason for the re-designing and the larger funnel is not apparent.
1899 Entered South America coastal service. Valparaiso-Arica-Mollendo-Callao.
1921 Placed on Valparaiso-Cristobal service.
1923 Sold to James y Cia, Valparaiso; renamed *Fresia*.
1935 Taken over by Soc. Anon. Maritima Chilena, Valparaiso.
1949 Broken up.

130 TALCA (II)

B 1900 Robert Napier & Sons, Glasgow; **T:**1,081g, 789n.
D 209ft 11in (63.98m) x 35ft 1in (10.69m) x 15ft 7in (4.75m).
E Tw scr, tpl exp; 2 x 3 cyl; 10 kts; By builder.
H Steel, 2 decks.
1900 Entered Pacific local coastal services.
1901 July 12: Wrecked off Puchoco Point, Chile.

POTOSI (II), GALICIA (II)

131 POTOSI (II)

B 1900 Wigham Richardson & Co., Newcastle; **T:**5,300g, 3,310n.
D 400ft 6in (122.07m) x 50ft (15.24m) x 33ft 4in (10.16m).
E Tw scr, tpl exp; 2 x 3 cyl; 411 HP; 13 kts; By builder.
H Steel, 3 decks. **P** 24 2nd, 338 3rd (Licensed for 780). Crew: 61.
1900 Built for Valparaiso service but sold upon completion due to a lack of trade. Renamed *Kazan*, Russian Volunteer Fleet.
1904 Captured by the Japanese; became *Kasato Maru*, Navy Department.
1918 To Osaka Shosen K. K.; same name, later spelled *Kasado Maru*.
1930 Broken up in Japan.

132 GALICIA (II)
Details as *Potosi* (131) except:- **B** 1901; **T:**5,896g, 3,796n.
1901 Built for Liverpool-Valparaiso route but completed without passenger accommodation being installed.
1915 July 31: mined in the English Channel in the Downs; reached port safely.
1917 May 12: mined again off Teignmouth and sank.

PERICO

133 PERICO
B 1901 J. Jones & Sons, Birkenhead; **T:**268g, 21n.
D 125ft 6in (38.25m) x 23ft 1in (7.04m) x 9ft 5in (2.86m).
E Tw scr, compound; 2 x 2 cyl; 65 HP; 9 kts; By builder.
H Steel, 1 deck and shade deck.
1901 Tender at Panama; replaced *Morro* (100).
1924 Out of Service

PANAMA (III), VICTORIA, MEXICO, CALIFORNIA

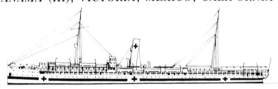
MAINE

134 PANAMA (III)
B 1902 Fairfield S B & E Co., Glasgow; **T:**5,981g, 3,507n.
D 401ft 2in (122.28m) x 52ft 4in (15.95m) x 33ft 8in (10.26m).
E Tw scr, tpl exp; 2 x 3 cyl; 550 NHP; 13½ kts; By builder. Coal: 1304 tons at 78.33 per day.
H Steel, 2 decks, shade deck and promenade deck; F: 63ft (19.2m).
P 106 1st, 104 2nd, 595 3rd. Crew: 123.
1902 Mar 8: Launched. May: Entered service Liverpool-Valparaiso then, later, transferred with the remainder of the class to the coastal route.
1914-18 Served as a hospital ship.
1918 Nov: Repatriated German prisoners of war.
1919 Repatriated wounded and troops from the Eastern Mediterranean.
1920 Became the Admiralty's permanent hospital ship (as drawn) *Maine*.
1922 May 24: Took up station at Malta.
1924 Based at Constantinople.
1927 Jan to Nov: China Station.
1935 Hotel ship for 500 Government guests at the Silver Jubilee of King George V.
1936 Based at Alexandria during the Abyssinian War. Then at Haifa during the Palestine troubles.

1937-8 During the Spanish Civil War *Maine* steamed 20,996 miles and evacuated 6,574 refugees of 41 nationalities.
1939 Was Internationally numbered '1' as the oldest hospital ship afloat.
1941 Sept 6: Bombed at Alexandria; 4 killed.
1945 At Piraeus during the Greek Civil War.
1946 Oct 22: When the British destroyers *Saumarez* and *Volage* struck Albanian mines in the Corfu Channel, killing 45, *Maine* went to the scene — grounding severely as she did so.
1947 Feb 21: Paid off at Rosyth.
1948 July 8: Arrived at Barrow for breaking up.
Note: The Italian liner *Leonardo da Vinci*, captured when Italy surrendered in 1943, was firstly renamed *Empire Clyde* and in 1946 *Maine*.

135 VICTORIA

Details as *Panama* (134) except: **B** 1902. **T**:5,967g, 3,742n.
1902 June 21: Launched.
1903 Mar 5: Maiden voyage to Valparaiso then straight onto the Callao run. Drawing has bridge forward. Later this class had the bridge repositioned as in *Panama/Maine*. Note two small side derricks for handling gangways; this was common to the coastal express ships. After the war white painted canvas was introduced along the main deck rails.
1914-18 Government service.
1923 Broken up in Holland.

136 MEXICO

Details as *Panama (134) except:-* **B** 1902; **T**:5,549g, 2,994n. Pass: 130 1st.
1902 Mar 22: Launched. July 2: Operated PSNC's first Norwegian Fjord cruise with 114 passengers. July 30: placed on South American routes.
1917 Mar 23: mined or torpedoed in the bows during the passage through the English Channel. Saved from sinking by steaming astern all the way into the nearest port. The damage was minimised by using cotton bales to plug the hole.
1922 Broken up.

137 CALIFORNIA

Details as *Panama* (134) except:- **B** 1902; **T**:5,547g, 2,991n.
1902 June 21: Launched on the same day as *Victoria*. Oct 2: Maiden sailing was Liverpool-Valparaiso-Callao then Valparaiso-Callao.
1917 Oct 17: Torpedoed off Cape Vilano; 4 lives lost.

RUPANCO

138 **RUPANCO**
B 1895 Howaldtswerke, Kiel; **T**:818g, 638n.

D 182ft (55.47m) x 32ft (9.75m) x 17ft 6in (5.33m).
E Tw scr, compound; 2 x 2 cyl; 80 NHP; 9 kts; By Ross and Duncan, constructed in 1890.
H Steel, 2 decks; B: 46ft (14.02m).
1895 Built for Ferdinand Prehn, (also spelled Prein), Kiel.
1902 Acquired to replaced the lost *Talca* (130). Voyaged out to Valparaiso.
1914 Sank at Valparaiso.

139 GALLITO

B 1902 J. Shearer & Son, Glasgow; **T**:130g, 69n.
D 86ft (26.21m) x 19ft (5.79m) x 8ft 10in (2.68m).
E Sgl scr, compound; 2 cyl; 23 RHP; kts; By Hutson & Son, Glasgow.
H Steel, 1 deck.
1902 Tug in South American waters. The name means 'Little Rooster'.
1931 Sold and broken up.

ORITA

140 ORITA (I)

B 1903 Harland & Wolff, Belfast; **T**:9,266g, 5,824n, 11,200 dwt.
D 485ft 5in (147.95m) x 58ft (17.68m) x 39ft 4in (11.99m).
E Tw scr, quad exp; 2 x 4 cyl; 1,148 HP; Stm P: 215 lb; 3 dbl and 3 sgl ended boilers, 27 furnaces; 14 kts; By builder. Coal: 1493 tons at 94 per day.
H Steel, 3 decks and Orlop deck; F: 53ft (16.15m).
P 169 1st, 111 2nd, 528 3rd. Crew: 172.
1902 Nov 15: Launched. The largest liner on the route at this date.
1903 Apr 8: Maiden voyage Liverpool-Valparaiso-Callao, her regular berth.
1919 Feb 10: Took the second P.S.N.C. sailing Liverpool-Panama Canal-Callao-Valparaiso. But the East coast route via Montevideo was more profitable and predominated.
1927 Sept 22: Made her final sailing via Montevideo than laid up in UK.
1931 Broken up at Morecambe, Lancashire. A typical example of good uneventful service.

141 POTOSI (III)

B 1905 W. Pickersgill & Sons, Sunderland; **T**:4,375g, 3,155n, 7,300 dwt.
D 381ft 5in (116.26m) x 49ft (14.93m) x 25ft 8in (7.82m).
E Sgl scr, tpl exp; 3 cyl; 429 HP: Stm P: 180 lb; 2 sgl ended boilers, 6 furnaces; 12 kts; By G. Clark, Sunderland.

H Steel, 2 decks and shelter deck. 4 hatches 24ft (7.31m) x 16ft (4.88m). Cargo: 306,000 cu ft (8,660 cu m); Fuel: 502 tons coal at 42 tons per day.
P 12 2nd, 397 3rd in dormitories.
1905 Entered PSNC general cargo service.
1914 The first British ship to transit the Panama Canal.
1925 Sold; became *Georgios M* of N. Kulukundis, Syra, Greece.
1927 Owners E. G. Culucundis and S. C. Costomeni, Syra. New boilers; Stm P: 140 lb.
1929 Owners became S. G. Lyras and M. G. Lemos.
1931 Nov 9: En route Varna-Antwerp with a cargo of grain her cargo shifted in a storm. *PLM 22* rescued 5 men but was driven off and *Georgios M* was not seen again; 18 lives lost.

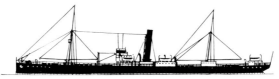

DUENDES, ESMERÁLDAS, BOGOTA (II), FLAMENCO (I)

142 DUENDES

Details as *Potosi* (141) except:- **B** 1906 Sir Jaimes Laing & Sons, Sunderland; **T:**4,602g, 2,948n.
D and **E** as *Bogota* (14).
1906 Entered service. Cargo ship.
1914-18 Munitions transport.
1916 March 25: Survived being shelled by a U-boat 70 miles W of Scillies.
1927 Sold; renamed *Zachariosa*, G. Lykiardopulo, Greece.
1932 Broken up.

143 ESMERALDAS

Details as *Potosi* (141) except:- **B** 1906 Sir James Laing & Sons, Sunderland; **T:**4,491g, 2,882n.
D and **E** as *Bogota* (142).
1906 Entered service. Cargo vessel.
1916 Transported 600 mules from Buenos Aires to Mombasa for the East African campaign.
1917 Captured and sunk by the German Armed Merchant Cruiser *Möewe*.

144 BOGOTA (II)

Details as *Potosi* (141) except:- **B** 1906 Sir James Laing & Sons, Sunderland; **T:**4,603g, 2,949n.
D 390ft (118.87m) x 50ft (15.24m) x 28ft 5in (8.66m).
1906 Entered service. Cargo ship.
1916 Nov 10: Sunk by torpedo in the North Atlantic.

145 FLAMENCO (I)

Details as *Potosi* (141) except:- **B** 1906 Sir James Laing & Sons, Sunderland; **T:**4,540g, 2,903n.

D and **E** as *Bogota* (142).
1906 Delivered for South American cargo services.
1916 Feb 6: Stopped 310 miles north west of Pernambuco by the German Armed Merchant cruiser *Möewe*. Sunk by time bombs; 1 killed.

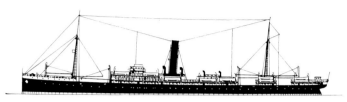

ORTEGA, ORIANA, ORONSA

146 **ORTEGA (I)**

B 1906 Harland & Wolff, Belfast; **T:** 7,970g, 4,519n.
D 482ft (146.91m) oa, 465ft 4in (141.83m) x 56ft 4in (17.17m) x 35ft 11in (10.95m).
E Tw scr, quad exp; 2 x 4 cyl; 1,125 HP; Stm P: 215 lb; 3 dbl and 3 sgl ended boilers, 27 furnaces; 15½ kts; By builder. Coal: 2,300 tons at 120 per day.
H Steel, 3 decks; **F:** 86ft (26.21m). 14 derricks, 13 winches.
P 160 1st, 128 2nd, 300 3rd plus 500 emigres in 'tween deck dormitories. Crew: 177
1906 March 22: Launched. July 19: Maiden voyage to Callao. This vessel introduced the Bibby tandem cabin (giving all passengers a porthole) to the route.
1914 Aug 4: When war was declared with Germany *Ortega*, Captain Douglas Kinnier, was at Montevideo en route for Callao.
Sept 16: She put to sea from Valparaiso for Liverpool and was chased by the German cruiser *Dresden*.
Sept 19: When ordered to stop *Ortega* turned and entered the uncharted Nelson Strait near Cape Horn. *Dresden* waited for *Ortega* to re-appear, but led by two ship's boats sounding as they went the liner traversed 100 miles via the landward side of the Queen Adelaide Archipelago and made Smyth Channel and the Straits of Magellan. There she was met by the Chilean warship *Admiral Lynch* which was searching for survivors.
1918 Used to transport American troops to France.
1919 Jan 31: Took the first sailing to Valparaiso via the Panama Canal.
1924 Dec 4: Reverted to the southern route to Chile.
1927 Sold for £19,500 and broken up at Briton Ferry.

147 **ORIANA**

Details as *Ortega* (146) except:- **B** 1906 Barclay Curle & Co., Glasgow; **T:**8,086g, 4,532n.
This ship had no derrick post vents in front of the bridge.
1906 Apr 26: Launched. June 21: Maiden voyage to Callao, southern route.
1915-19 Government service; predominantly trooping.
1918 May 8: While in convoy went aground in dense fog on Torcor Head by Rathlin Island. It was an incredible event. The escorting destroyers *Martial* and *Nicator* were also aground and with the lifting of the fog Alfred Holt's *Aeneas* and *Manora* of British India could be seen well ashore on the (fortunately) shelving rocks. All were off within two weeks.
1919 Oct 17: Resumed commercial service.
1922 Nov: Transferred to the Panama Canal route.
1927 Broken up.

148 **ORONSA**

Details as *Ortega* (146) except:- **T**:7,989g, 4,516n.

Identification: The lifeboat abaft the Bridge was slung not nested on deck — which ended at the after end of the bridge house.

1906 May 26: Launched. Sept 13: Entered service with an additional call at Pernambuco en-route.

1918 Apr 28: Torpedoed off Bardsey Island whilst in convoy on a bright moonlit night. Her boilers blew up and the ship sank with the loss of 3 lives.

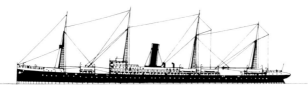

CALLAO (II)

149 **CALLAO (II)**

B 1885 Harland & Wolff, Belfast; **T**:4,206g, 2,691n.

D 420ft 4in (128.12m) x 42ft 50in (12.93m) x 29ft 4in (8.94m)

E Sgl scr, 2 tandem compound inverted, 4 cyl, 500 HP; Stm P 70lb. 14 Kts. By builder. Coal: 697 tons at 65 tons per day.

H Iron. 3 dks.

P 83 1st, 44 2nd, 280 3rd. Crew: 104.

1885 Feb 28: Launched for White Star Line as *Gaelic* (II) for Pacific work.

July 18: Maiden voyage Liverpool-New York thence round to San Francisco on charter to Occidental & Oriental Steamship Co, San Francisco.

Nov 10: First sailing to Yokohama and Hong Kong.

1904 Dec 13: Final sailing from San Francisco.

1905 March: Sold to P.S.N.C; renamed *Callao*. Pacific coast route pending the arrival of *Quillota* (154).

1907 Sept: Broken up at Briton Ferry, South Wales.

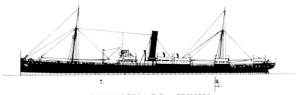

HUANCHACO, JUNIN

150 **HUANCHACO**

B 1907 W. Beardmore & Co., Glasgow; **T**:4,524g, 2,840n. 7,200 dwt.

D 390ft 7in (119.05m) x 50ft 2in (15.29m) x 25ft 8in (7.82m).

E Sgl scr, tpl exp; 2 x 3; 463 HP; Stm P: 190 lb; 3 sgl ended boilers, 12 furnaces; 10 kts; By builder.

H Steel, 2 decks and shelter deck. Fuel: 1,077 tons coal.

P 18 2nd, 726 3rd in dormitories fore and aft. Crew: 47.

1907 Aug: Entered cargo service.

1914 Aug: Became a Government transport mainly horses and stores.

1919 Returned to P.S.N.C.

1925 Sold; renamed *Frank Sutton*.

1926 Became *Bore VIII*, Aktiebolaget Bore, Abo, Finland.

1929 Broken up.

151 JUNIN

Details as *Huanchaco* (150) except:- T:4,536g, 2,846n.
D 391ft 6in (119.18m).
1907 Sept: Entered cargo service.
1926 Sold; became *Cambrian Idylle*, William Thomas Shipping Co., Liverpool.
1929 Broken up.

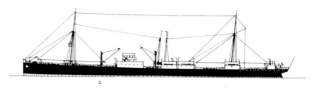

KENUTA (I), LIMA (III)

152 KENUTA (I)

B 1907 John Brown & Co., Glasgow; **T**:4,953g, 3,134n, 7,615 dwt.
D 401ft 4in (122.33m) x 52ft 2in (15.9m) x 25ft 8in (7.82m).
E Sgl scr, tpl exp; 3 cyl; 485 HP; Stm P: 180lb; 3 sgl ended boilers, 12 furnaces; 10 kts;
By builder.
H Steel, 2 decks; Fuel: 1,077 tons coal. 20 derricks, 10 winches.
P 33 2nd, 250 3rd. Crew: 57. Fitted for emigrant dormitories fore and aft: 693 souls.
1907 Oct: Entered service.
1926 Sold and renamed *Vasilios Pandelis*, Pandelis Bros.
1930 Managed by Constants (South Wales) Ltd., Cardiff.
1933 Broken up in Italy.

153 LIMA (III)

Details as *Kenuta* (152) except:- T:4,946g, 3,130n.
1907 Dec: Delivered.
1910 Feb 10: Wrecked in the Straits of Magellan on Huamblin Island during a severe gale; Captain Percy Jacob. S.S. *Hatumet* (Hathor S S Co., London) stood by and rescued 188 passengers and 17 crew. During this operation 6 crew were drowned when a lifeboat capsized. There were 88 persons still aboard. The overloaded *Hatumet* steamed into Ancud and the Chilean cruiser *Blanca Encalada* raced back and took off the remaining 88 survivors.

QUILLOTA, QUILPUE

154 QUILLOTA

B 1907 Wm Beardmore & Co., Glasgow; **T**:3,674g, 1,958n.
D 361ft 5in (110.16m) x 46ft 2in (14.07m) x 22ft 2in (6.73m).
E Tw scr, tpl exp; 2 x 3; 550 HP; Stm P: 190 lb; 4 sgl ended boilers, 12 furnaces; 14 kts;
By builder.
H Steel, 2 decks. **P** 120 1st, 100 2nd, 300 deck.
1907 Feb: Built for Valparaiso-Callao service.
1915 Chartered by Royal Mail to replace *Berbice*, on war service.

1921 Operated on New York-Panama Canal-Guayaquil route.
1923 Sold to Soc. Anon. Maritima Chilena; renamed *Chile*. Rebuilt with lifeboats raised and superstructure increased to resemble *Peru* (124).
1928 Joined by *Peru* (124) on Chilean coastal routes. Yellow funnel, black top, broad black band.
1931 Out of service.

155 QUILPUE

Details as *Quillota* (154) except:- **T**:3,669g, 1,959n.
1907 May: Entered service for Valparaiso-Callao service.
1915 Chartered by Royal Mail to replace *Balantia*, on war service.
1917 June 12: Attacked by U-boat gunfire. Her own gun drove off the enemy.
1921 Placed on New York-Panama Canal-Guayaquil service.
1922 Sold; renamed *Gascoyne*, West Australian S.N. Co.; Bethell Gwyn & Co. managers, Liverpool.
1930 Broken up.

156 EXPLORER

B 1873 Liverpool; **T**: 2,066g, 1,437n.
D 300ft 4in (91.54m) x 34ft 8in (10.57m) x 25ft 2in (7.67m).
E Sgl scr, compound; 2 cyl; 9 kts. **H** Iron
1873 Built as *Crocus* but not recorded in Lloyds Register; renamed *Explorer*, T. & J. Harrison.
1907 Acquired by PSNC; same name. The last iron hulled vessel to join the fleet.
1914 Hulked.

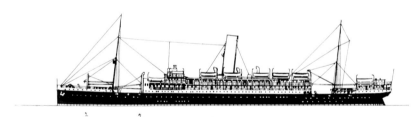

ORCOMA

157 ORCOMA (I)

B 1908 Wm Beardmore & Co., Dalmuir, Glasgow; **T**:11,546g, 7,086n. 10,210dwt.
D 511ft 7in (115.93m) x 62ft 2in (18.95m) x 29ft 1in (8.86m).
E Tw scr, quad exp; 2 x 4 cyl; 7,100 IHP; 1,342NHP; Stm P: 210 lb; 3 dbl and 3 sgl ended boilers, 36 furnaces; 14½ kts; By builder. Coal: 2,847 tons.
H Steel, 2 decks and shelter deck; F:93ft (28.35m); B:243ft (74.07m); P:50ft (15.24m). 23 derricks, 12 winches.
P 246 1st, 202 2nd, 106 intermediate, 456 3rd. Crew 247.
1908 Apr 2: Launched.
Aug 27: Maiden voyage Liverpool-Magellan-West coast of South America. The largest and fastest vessel on the South American Pacific route.
1909 Took the first Thomas Cook conducted tour to South America at £300 per person.
1914 Took outbound record Liverpool-Callao in 32 days 22 hours 40 minutes including ports of call, via the Straits of Magellan.

Oct: Returned to UK in a faster time missing the holocaust of the German victory at Coronel by a few hours.

1915 Mar: Served as an Armed Merchant Cruiser on Northern patrol with 10th Cruiser Squadron. 6 x 6in (15.24cm) and 2 x 6 pounder guns.

1919 Nov 7: Reverted to PSNC service; first post war commercial voyage with northbound via Panama Canal and New York.

1923 Converted to oil fuel. Well deck aft plated over. Modernised.

1933 June: Broken up at Blyth by Hughes Bolckow having been replaced by *Reina del Pacifico* (190). She fetched £14,580.

PODEROSO

158 **PODEROSO**

B 1911 H & C. Grayson, Liverpool; **T**:285g, 115n.

D 115ft 4in (35.14m) x 25ft 1 in (7.65m) x 13ft 2in (4.01m).

E Sgl scr, tpl exp; 3 cyl; 103 NHP; Stm P; 160 lb; 1 sgl ended boiler, 3 furnaces; 9 kts; By Crabtree & Co., Great Yarmouth. **H** Steel, 1 deck.

Although the deep sea vessels by now carried yellow funnels tugs still appear with buff upperworks and black funnels.

1911 Tug. Various South American stations. The Buenos Aires & Pacific Railway Co. owned a smaller tug with the same name which attended P.S.N.C. vessels at Buenos Aires; the cause of some confusion.

1938/9 Sold to Chile. Disposal not known.

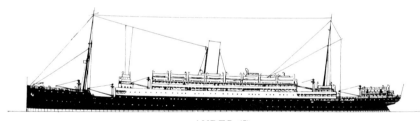

ANDES (I)

159 **ANDES (I)**

B 1913 Harland & Wolf, Belfast. **T**:15,620g, 9,481n.

D 570ft (173.84m) x 67.3ft (20.52m) x 43ft (13.11m).

E Tpl scr, tpl exp with one exhaust low pressure turbine connected to the centre shaft, 2 x 4 cyl; 14,000 IHP, 17 kts. By builder.

H Steel. 3 dks. **P** 380 1st, 250 2nd, 700 3rd. Deck cranes in pairs.

Completed with 2 x 4.7in (11.94cm) guns right aft.

1913 May 8: Launched. Intended for PSNC but transferred to Royal Mail on the stocks. Sept 26: Maiden voyage for PSNC Liverpool-Valparaiso, then Southampton-River Plate service for Royal Mail.

1915 Apr: Converted to Armed Merchant Cruiser. 8 x 6in (15.24cm) guns; 2 x 6 pounders, plus depth charges.

1916 Feb 29: With her sister ship *Alcantara* (144) engaged the German raider *Greif* (masquerading as the Norwegian *Rena)*. Although *Greif* was sunk *Alcantara* was herself sunk and *Andes* picked up the survivors including 115 Germans.

1917 Atlantic convoy work. Then repatriated British submarine crews trapped by the Soviet Revolution at Murmansk.

1919 Jan: Reconditioned at Belfast, resumed the River Plate Run in Oct.
1929 Converted at Gladstone Dock, Liverpool, to cruising liner, painted white; renamed *Atlantis*. Pass: 450 1st. Converted to oil fuel. A swimming pool was installed behind the bridge.
1935 Attended Silver Jubilee Naval Review at Spithead.
1939 Aug: At Danzig on a cruise when recalled. Aug 25: Reached Southampton. Converted into hospital ship *No 33* with 400 beds. 130 Medical staff joined. Initially based at Alexandria.
1940 Apr: Returned to Norwegian waters for the Norwegian evacuation campaign. Bombed twice. Sept: Indian Ocean work for two years.
1942 Took part in Madagascar operation; based at Diego Suarez.
1943 Used for the repatriation of prisoners of war. Took Italians to Lisbon and Germans to Gothenburg.
1944-46 Hospital and repatriation duties. Steamed 280,000 miles and carried 35,000 wounded.
1948 Chartered for 4 years to carry emigrants from Southampton to Australia and New Zealand. Pass: 900 3rd.
1952 Laid up in the Clyde then sold for scrapping at Faslane.

160 **CALBUCO**

B 1913 Lytham S.B. & E. Co., Lytham, Lancashire; **T**:55g, 27n.
D 62ft 2in (18.95m) x 15ft 1in (4.6m) x 7ft 5in (2.25m).
E Sgl scr, compound; 2 cyl; 14RHP; Stm P: 130 lb; 1 sgl ended boiler, 1 furnace; 9 kts; By builder.
H Steel, 1 deck.
1913 Aug: Steam tug for barges to replenish coal hulks.
1925 Sold.

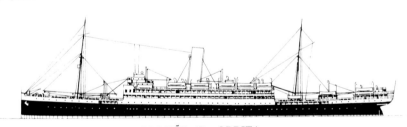

ORDUÑA (I), ORBITA

161 **ORMEDA/ORDUÑA (I)**

B 1914 Harland & Wolff, Belfast; **T**:15,507g, 9,548n, 12,370 dwt.
D 570ft (173.74m) oa, 550ft 4in (167.64m) x 67ft 4in (20.52m) x 43ft (13.11m); Dft 32ft 6in (9.91m) to give 25,230 tons displacement.
E Tpl scr, tpl exp exhausting to a direct acting turbine connected to the centre shaft; 2 x 4 cyl; 8,650 IHP; 1,362 NHP; Stm P: 215 lb; 6 dbl ended boilers and 36 furnaces; 15 kts; By builder. The turbine had no reverse gearing.
H Steel, 4 decks.
Cargo: 9,324 tons. Fuel: 2,272 tons coal. 23 derricks, 19 winches.
P 194 1st, 217 2nd, 154 Intermediate, 564 3rd.
1913 Oct 2: Launched as *Orduña* (pronounced Ordunya). Originally intended to be named *Ormeda*.
1914 Feb 19: Maiden voyage to Valparaiso. Her funnel was then black. Oct: Chartered to Cunard for Liverpool-New York service to replace vessels called up for

trooping. Carried Cunard funnel when not grey painted. Nov 1: First Cunard sailing.
1915 June 28: Chased by U-boat, but outran the attacker 20 miles from the Smalls.
1915 July 9: Missed by a torpedo 30 miles S. of Queenstown (Cobh).
1918 June: Sank a German submarine by gunfire. Dec 1: Collided with and sank Elder Dempster's *Konakry* off Galley Head, Ireland.
1919 Dec 31: With the ending of the Cunard charter returned to P.S.N.C.
1920 Apr 1: Resumed service via Montevideo.
1921 Operated Royal Mail Line's Hamburg-Southampton-New York service. May 28: First sailing. Catered for the lack of German berths.
1922 Autumn refit by builders.
1923 Jan 1: Resumed South American service. **P** 190 1st, 221 2nd, 476 3rd. Ownership transferred to Royal Mail Line.
1926 Converted to oil fuel. **P** 234 1st, 186 2nd, 458 3rd.
1927 Reverted to P.S.N.C. ownership Apr 7: Panama Canal route.
1941 Taken over as a troopship.
1946 Government trooping service. Boat deck derrick posts removed prior to this.
1950 Nov: Decommissioned and laid up.
1951 Broken up at Dalmuir after 37 years exemplary service.

162 **ORBITA (I)**

Details as *Orduña* (161) except: **T**:15,495g, 10,140n.
P 190 1st, 221 2nd, 476 3rd.
1914 July 7: Launched. Provision for 6 x 6in (15.24cm) guns was made.
1915 Entered service as an auxiliary cruiser. Later used as a short crossing troopship.
1919 Mar: Completion work commenced. Sept 26: Maiden voyage southbound.
1921 Apr 30: Chartered to Royal Mail for Hamburg-Southampton-New York.
1923 Transferred with her sistership to Royal Mail ownership.
1926 Fitted to burn oil fuel. Returned to P.S.N.C. and their routes. Nov 4: Liverpool-Panama Canal-Callao-Valparaiso.
1941 Troopship duties for the duration of the war. Boat deck posts out.
1946 Emigrant service to the Antipodes.
1950 Broken up by Thos. W. Ward at Newport, Monmouthshire.

JAMAICA

163 **JAMAICA**

B 1908 W. Harkess & Son, Middlesbrough; **T**:1,138g, 602n.
D 220ft (67.06m) x 34ft (10.36m) x 14ft 11in (4.52m).
E Sgl scr, tpl exp; 3 cyl; 171 NHP; Stm P: 180 lb; 2 sgl ended boilers, 4 furnaces. 11 kts; By McColl & Pollock, Sunderland.
H Steel, 2 decks; F: 28ft (8.53m), B: 79ft (24.08m) P: 24ft (7.31m).
1908 Built for Imperial Direct West India Service, Elder Dempster & Co.
1914 Acquired for Central American services; same name.
1915 Requisitioned for Government service.
1918 Shown as owned by Royal Mail Line but did not return to their service. Reverted to PSNC service.
1929 Sold; renamed *Coyhaique*, Soc. Industrial del Aysen, Valparaiso.
1943 Broken up.

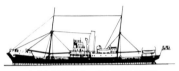

ACAJUTLA, SALVADOR

164 ACAJUTLA

B 1911 Swan Hunter & Wigham Richardson, Wallsend; **T:** 1,170g, 654n.
D 215ft 8in (65.74m) x 33ft 6in (10.21m) x 19ft 5in (5.92m).
E Sgl scr, tpl exp; 3 cyl: 17in (43.18cm), 28in (71.12cm) and 46 in (116.84cm); Stroke: 33in (83.82cm); 174 HP; 2 sgl ended boilers; 11 kts; By builder.
H Steel, 1 deck of teak; **F:** 27ft (8.23cm).
1911 Built for Salvador Railway Company, London.
1915 Acquired with *Salvador* (165) for Central American services; same name, fortnightly service through the Panama Canal.
192? Rebuilt and modernised; illustration 164a.
1946 Sold; renamed *Marathon*, Pandelis Line, Greece but operated initially by Neil and Pandelis, London. Greek Islands service.

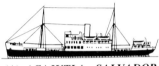

(A) ACAJUTLA, SALVADOR

165 SALVADOR

Details as *Acajutla* (164) except:- **B** 1909; **T:**1,128g, 637n.
1909 Built for Salvador Railway Company, London.
1915 Acquired for Central American services; same name.
192? Rebuilt and modernised 164a.
1946 Sold; renamed *Salamis*, Pandelis Line, Greece, but operated initially by Neil and Pandelis, London. Greek Islands services. At the time of her sale *Salvador* had made 779 transits of the Panama Canal; the greatest number by any commercial vessel. The Panama Canal Co issued a certificate in honour of the event. *Acajutla* (164) also received one.

CAUCA

166 CAUCA

B 1915 Swan Hunter & Wigham Richardson, Wallsend; **T:** 1,448g, 890n.
D 246ft (74.98m) x 35ft 2in (10.72m) x 20ft (6.1m).
E Sgl scr, tpl exp; 3 cyl; 193 NHP; 11 kts; By builder.
H Steel, 1 deck; **F:** 33ft (10.06m), **P:** 28ft (8.53m).
1915 Entered service, based Panama.
1923 Sold; renamed *Tonkin* Compagnie Indo-Chinoise de Navigation, Haiphong, Indo-China.
193? Sold.

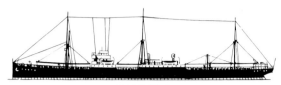

LAUTARO

167 **LAUTARO**

B 1915 Harland & Wolff, Glasgow; **T:**6,240g, 3,950n.

D 399ft 1in (121.64m) x 52ft 2in (15.9m) x 33ft 10in (10.31m).

E Tw scr, oil; 4 stroke sgl acting; 12 cyl; 719 NHP; 12 kts; By Burmeister and Wain, Glasgow.

H Steel, 2 decks and awning deck. **P** 12.

1915 Dec: Built as *Bostonian*, Leyland Line.

1916 Sold to Glen Line, London; renamed *Glengyle*.

1917 June 10: Chased by submarine in Mediterranean. Used gunfire to escape.

1923 Acquired by PSNC, became *Lautaro*.

1947 Sold to Jenny S. S. Co., London; renamed *River Swift*.

1948 Caught fire at Rio de Janeiro, written off as beyond repair.

1949 Broken up in South America.

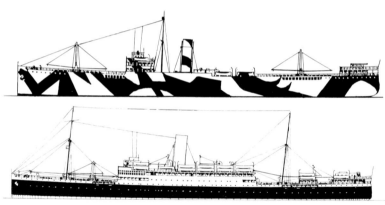

ORCA (A) ORCA

168 **ORCA**

B 1918 Harland & Wolff, Belfast; **T:** 15,120g, 9,614n, 11,380 dwt.

D 574ft (174.96m) oa, 550ft 4in (167.74m) x 67ft 4in (20.52m) x 43ft (13.11m).

E Tpl scr, tpl exp exhausting to a direct geared, forward drive only, turbine connected to the centre shaft. 4 cyl; 1,362 HP; Stm P: 215 lb; 6 dbl ended boilers with 36 furnaces; 15 kts; By builder. The engine installation was identical to that of *Orduña* (161) and *Orbita* (162). She was planned as a cruiser sterned sister vessel.

H Steel, 3 decks with a 4th deck fore and aft of the machinery space. Boat deck 230ft (70.1m); 10 bulkheads, 6 holds.

P 1918: Nil 1922: 190 1st, 220 2nd, 480 3rd.

1918 Jan 15: Launched. Completed as a cargo carrier (168).

1921 Feb 18: Arrived at builder's for completion as designed.

1922 Dec 18: After completion as a passenger liner made her first sailing Southampton-Hamburg-New York (168a).

1923 Transferred to Royal Mail Line ownership.

1927 Jan: Sold to White Star Line service; renamed *Calgaric*. T:16,063g, 9,614n. Pass: 290 1st, 550 tourist, 330 3rd.

May 4: First voyage Liverpool-Quebec-Montreal. Pass: 100 cabin, 500 3rd.
1931 Laid up at Milford Haven, made one cruise to the Baltic with Boy Scouts.
1933 June 9: Commenced a summer season of voyages Liverpool-Montreal.
Sept 9: Laid up at Milford Haven again.
1934 Sold for £31,000 and scrapped at Rosyth during 1935. The ship was only 16 years old.

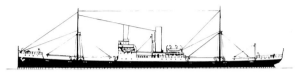

BALLENA, BOGOTA (III)

169 BALLENA

B 1919 W. Dobson & Co., Newcastle; **T:**5,210g, 3,216n, 8,075 dwt.
D 400ft 1in (121.95m) x 52ft 4in (15.95m) x 26ft 5in (8.05m).
E Sgl scr, tpl exp; 3 cyl; 452 NHP; 3 boilers; 11 kts; By North East Marine Eng. Co., Newcastle.
H Steel, 2 decks; F: 39ft (11.89m), B: 113ft (34.44m), P: 49ft (14.93m), Fuel: 490 tons coal. Crew 41.
1919 Nov 7: Launched as a wartime standard "B" type vessel.
1920 Entered service as *Ballena* for PSNC.
1933 Sold; renamed *Mount Ida*, Rethymnis & Kulukundis, Panama.
1937 Mar: Became *Mendoza*, Hamburg Sud Amerika Line, Hamburg.
1940 Dec 8: Collided off Flushing with *Adalia*, Hamburg America.
1945 Mar 22: Sunk by Russian bombers off Pillau.

170 BOGOTA (III)

Details as *Ballena* (169) except:- **B:** Cammell Laird & Co., Birkenhead; **T:**5,167g. 3,127n.
1919 Mar 18: Launched as *War Lapwing*. Renamed *Bogota* before commissioning.
1932 Sold; renamed *Madda*, Fratelli G & F Bozzo, Genoa.
1937 June 17: damaged during the Spanish Civil War.
1940 June: chased by British warships, beached at Tenerife and later refloated.
1945 Became *Monte Nafarrate*, Cia Nav. Sota y Aznar (Sir Ramon de la Sota), Bilbao, Spain.
1956 Renamed *Riva de Luna*, Angel Riva Suardiaz, Bilbao.
1958 Name changed to *Rivadeluna*, same owner.
1972 Owner: Naviera Rivadeluna.
1974 Broken up.

MAGELLAN (III)

171 MAGELLAN (III)

B 1913 J. C. Tecklenborg, Geestemunde; **T:**6,553g. 4,055n
D 462ft 4in (140.92m) x 59ft 2in (18.03m) x 28ft (8.53m).

E Sgl scr, quad exp; 4 cyl; 723 NHP; 3,700 IHP; 4 sgl ended boilers, 12 furnaces; 12 kts; By builder.
H Steel, 2 decks and shelter deck; F: 52ft (15.85m). Cargo: 635,000 cu ft (17.970 cu m); Fuel: 1,310 tons coal.
1913 Built as *Alda,* Roland Linie A.G., Bremen.
1919 Surrendered to Great Britain, Shipping Controller, managed by PSNC.
1920 Sold to PSNC; renamed *Magellan.*
1934 Broken up.

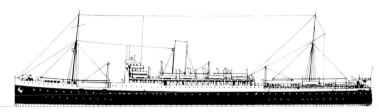

OROPESA (II)

172 **OROPESA (II)**
B 1920 Cammell Laird, Birkenhead; **T:**14,118g, 8,608n, 14,000 dwt.
D 530ft (161.54m) x 66ft 4in (20.22m) x 41ft 2in (12.55m). Dft: 34ft 5in (10.49m).
E Tw scr, 6 turbines, dbl reduction geared; 1,647 NHP, 7,500 IHP; 6 dbl ended boilers; 14½ kts; By builder.
H Steel, 2 decks and shelter deck: Cargo: 528,000 cu ft (14,942 cu m);
P 141 1st, 131 2nd, 360 3rd.
1919 Dec 9: launched.
1920 Sept 4: maiden voyage Liverpool-Rio de Janeiro-Buenos Aires.
1921 May 14: Chartered to Royal Mail for Hamburg-Southampton-New York service.
1922 Nov 30: Reverted to P.S.N.C. and the Valparaiso berth.
1924 Converted to oil fuel; capacity 3,500 tons.
1927 Feb: Moved onto the Panama Canal route to Valparaiso.
1931 Carried the Prince of Wales and Prince George to South America.
Oct: Laid up at Dartmouth for over six years.
1937 Back in service.
1939 Sept: Taken over for trooping duties.
1941 Jan 16: Torpedoed three times by *U-96* off Ireland; 113 dead.

LA PAZ, LOBOS, LOSADA

173 **LA PAZ**
B 1920 Harland & Wolff, Glasgow; **T:**6,548g, 4,052n.
D 406ft (123.85m) x 54ft 2in (16.51m) x 32ft 10in (10m).
E Tw scr, oil; 2 stroke, sgl acting; 12 cyls; 810 HP; 3,200 BHP; 12 kts; By builder.
H Steel, 2 decks and shelter deck; F: 45ft (13.72m), B: 89ft (27.13m), P: 32ft (9.75m); Cargo: 462,000 cu ft (13,074 cu m); Fuel: 11 tons oil per day.
1920 Entered service.
1942 May 1: Torpedoed by *U-109* off Florida with a cargo of export whisky, beached and then sold-cum-cargo to U.S. agents.
Later passed to War Shipping Administration.

1945 Sold to Construction Aggregates Corp., Chicago, Illinois. Not engaged in deep sea trading.
1954 Out of Lloyds.

174 **LOBOS**
Details as *La Paz* (173) except:- B 1921; T:6,479g, 3,997n.
1921 Entered service.
1952 Broken up.

175 **LOSADA**
Details as *La Paz* (173) except:- **B** 1921; T: 6,520g, 4,021n.
1921 Entered service. **1952** Broken up.

ALVARADO, ALMAGRO, ARANA

176 **ALVARADO**
B 1920 A & J Inglis, Glasgow; **T:**2,464g, 1,448n, 3860 dwt, 5,670 disp.
D 303ft 5in (92.48m) x 43ft (13.11m) x 20ft 8in (6.3m).
E Sgl scr, tpl exp; 3 cyls; 265 NHP; 2 dlb ended boilers, 6 furnaces; 10½ kts; By builder.
H Steel, 2 decks; F: 32ft (9.75m), B: 81ft (24.69m), P: 33ft (10.06m). Inset: 3-windowed bridge house lay out.
1920 Oct: completed as *War Raisin*. Acquired by MacAndrews & Co; renamed *Alvarado* for Mediterranean service. Proved to be too large.
1922 Acquired by PSNC; same name. Collier duties.
1933 Sold; became *Herval*, Cia. Carbonifera Rio-Grandense, Rio de Janeiro.
Continued in service as a collier.
1965 Broken up at Rio de Janeiro.

177 **ALMAGRO**
Details as *Alvarado* (176) except:- **T:**1,438n.
1920 Apr 23: Launched.
June 15: Completed as *Almagro* for MacAndrews & Co.,
1922 Acquired by PSNC; same name. New York-Valparaiso service.
1933 Sold; became *Itaquy*,Cia Carbonifera Rio-Grandense, Rio de Janeiro.
1934 Renamed *Tuquy*, same owner.
1963 Sold; renamed *Artico*.
1965 Became *Roma Um*, Comissario Maritima Modesta Roma, Rio de Janeiro.
1967 Feb: caught fire en route Manaus to Areia Branca. Beached at Belem.
Oct 30: Capsized and became a total loss.

178 **ARANA**
Details as *Alvarado* (176) except:- **T:**1,438n.
1919 Sept 17: Launched as *War Date*.
1920 Jan: Completed as *Arana* for MacAndrews & Co.
1922 Acquired by PSNC; same name. Collier New York-Valparaiso service.
1933 Sold; became *Chuy*, Cia. Carbonifera Rio-Grandense, Rio de Janeiro.
1943 To Cia. Commercio y Navegazione, Rio de Janeiro; same name.
1958 Sold to Nav. Mercantil S.A., Rio de Janeiro; same name.
1961 May: Broken up at Rio de Janeiro.

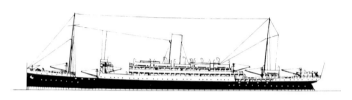

EBRO, ESSEQUIBO

179 **EBRO**
B 1915 Workman Clark & Co., Belfast; **T:**8,489g, 5,174n.
D 450ft 4in (137.26m) x 57ft 9in (17.6m) x 30ft 7in (9.32m).
E Tw scr, quad exp; 2 x 4 cyls; Stroke: 45in (114.3cm); 1,055 NHP; Stm P: 215 lb; 2 dbl and 2 sgl ended boilers, 24 furnaces.
H Steel, 2 decks; F: 71ft (21.64m), B: 218ft (66.45m), P: 78ft (23.77m).
P 250 1st, 250 3rd. Crew: 320.
1914 Sept 8: Launched for Royal Mail Line.
Apr 28: Maiden voyage to South America, then joined 10th Cruiser Squadron.
1922 Acquired by PSNC, same name; placed on New York-Panama Canal-Callao-Valparaiso service.
1930 Dec: Laid up in the River Dart.
1935 Feb: Sold to Jugoslavenska Lloyd; renamed *Princess Olga*. Cost £21,000.
1940 Became *Serpa Pinto*, Cia Colonial, Lisbon for Lisbon-New York and Central American service terminating at Rio de Janeiro.
1955 Broken up in Belgium. Her price was, by now, £115,000.

180 **ESSEQUIBO**
Details as *Ebro* (179) except:-
1914 July 6: Launched.
Nov 18: maiden voyage to South America, Captain J. C. Chevet.
1915 Taken over for use as a hospital ship.
1917 Stopped by *U-64*. Inspected, given "God speed you" and sent on her way.
1922 Acquired by PSNC; same name. Placed on New York-Panama Canal-Callao-Valparaiso service.
1930 Laid up.
1935 Mar: Sold to Arcos Ltd. for £21,000, transferred to USSR and renamed *Neva*.
1957 Taken out of Lloyds Register at the owner's request.

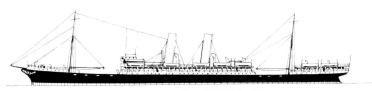

ORCANA (II), ORUBA (II)

181 **ORCANA (II)**

B 1903 Alex Stephen & Sons, Glasgow; T:6,793g, 3,691n.
D 454ft 10in (138.63m) x 55ft (16.76m) x 30ft (9.14m).
E Tw scr, tpl exp; 2 x 3 cyls; 1,218 NHP; Stm P: 200 lb; 2 dbl ended and 1 sgl ended boiler, 21 furnaces; 15 kts; By builder.
H Steel, 3 decks; F: 74ft (22.56m), B: 167ft (50.9m), P: 92ft (28.04m).
P 150 1st, 170 3rd.
1903 Built as *Miltiades* for Aberdeen line.
Nov 3: Maiden voyage London-Cape Town-Melbourne-Sydney.
1913 Lengthened to 504ft 4in (153.72m); T:7,814g, 4,892n.
B:217ft (66.14m). Second funnel, a dummy, added.
Pass: 89 1st, 158 3rd.
1915 Troopship.
1920 June 4: Resumed commercial service to Australia.
Nov 20: last departure from Australia. Then acquired by Royal Mail and renamed *Orcana*.
1922 Tranferred to PSNC.; same name. Replaced the 3 '*O's* transferred to the North Atlantic.
Aug 11: Placed on the intended 'Round South America' service. Liverpool-Montevideo-Valparaiso-Panama Canal-Liverpool. The ship had always been expensive to operate and on account of this the second sailing was cancelled. Laid up, firstly at Liverpool and then at Dartmouth.
1924 Towed to Holland and broken up at Hendrik-ido-Ambrecht.

182 **ORUBA (II)**

Details as *Orcana* (181) except:- **B** 1904; **T:** 6,795g, 3,695n.
1903 Nov 18: Launched for Aberdeen Line as *Marathon*
1904 Jan 27: Maiden voyage London-Cape Town-Melbourne-Sydney.
1912 Lengthened and modified as *Orcana*. T: 7,848g. Pass 90 1st, 150 3rd.
1915 Trooping duties.
1920 Oct 21: Reverted to Aberdeen service to Australia, made only one voyage. Sold to Royal Mail Line; renamed *Oruba*.
1921 Transferred to PSNC. May 26: Placed on South American service, 'Round America Service'.
1922 Laid up firstly in Liverpool then at Dartmouth.
1924 Broken up in Germany.

LAGUNA

183 **LAGUNA**

B 1923 Harland & Wolff, Glasgow; T:6,466g, 4,033n.

D 420ft 6in (128.17m) x 54ft 2in (16.51m) x 33ft 4in (10.16m).
E Tw scr, oil; 4 stroke sgl acting; 12 cyls: 832 NHP; 12 kts; By builder.
H Steel, 3 decks; F: 42ft (12.8m), B: 101ft (30.78m), P: 33ft (10.06m). **P** 12.
1923 Entered service via Panama Canal.
1952 Broken up at Barrow-in-Furness.

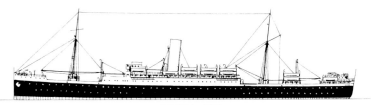

OROYA (III)

184 OROYA (III)
B 1923 Harland & Wolff, Belfast; **T:**12,257g, 7,380n.
D 525ft 4in (160.12m) x 62ft 9in (19.12m) x 44ft 7in (13.59m).
E Tw scr, 4 turbines, sgl reduction geared; Stm P. 215 lb; 4 dbl ended boilers, 24 furnaces; 14 kts; By builder.
H Steel, 2 decks and shelter deck; F: 55ft (16.76m), B: 217ft (66.14m)
P 150 1st, 123 2nd, 450 3rd.
1920 Dec 16: launched and laid up incomplete due to a lack of South American passenger traffic.
1923 Mar 22: maiden voyage Liverpool-Panama Canal-Valparaiso.
1931 Sept 8: Laid up at Dartmouth.
1938 Dec: Sold for breaking up to Italy.
1939 Feb 1: Left in tow of Smit's tug *Rode See* for La Spezia to be scrapped.

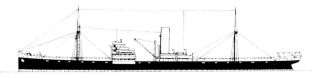

LORETO, LORIGA

185 LORETO
B 1919 Harland & Wolff, Glasgow; **T:**6,682g, 4,105n.
D 406ft 2in (123.8m) x 54ft 2in (16.51m) x 32ft 11in (10.03m).
E Tw scr, oil; 4 stroke sgl acting; 12 cyls; 12 kts; By builder.
H Steel, 2 decks and shelter deck; F: 48ft (14.63m), B: 81ft (24.69m), P 43ft (13.11m).
Lattice derricks. Those at No 3 hold are cross stowed.
1919 July: Built as *Glenade* for Glen Line, London.
1924 Acquired by PSNC.
1941 Feb 22: Under Captain Philip Hockey *Loreto*, by sailing into a fog bank, was the only ship in a convoy of six to escape destruction by the *Scharnhorst* and *Gneisenau* 400 miles off Newfoundland.
1951 Sold; renamed *Barbeta*, Motor Lines Ltd, Greenock.
1952 Nov: Broken up at Briton Ferry.

186 LORIGA
Details as *Loreto* (185) except:- **T:**6,665g, 4,051n.
1919 Built as *Glenariffe*, Glen Line, London.

1924 Acquired by PSNC; renamed *Loriga*.
1951 Sold; renamed *Oceanus Venus*, Ocean Transportation Co., Panama.
1953 Broken up in Japan.

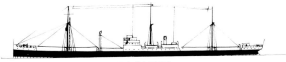

LAGARTO

187 **LAGARTO**

B 1915 Harland & Wolff, Glasgow; **T:** 5,075g, 3,208n.
D 385ft 1in (117.37m) x 52ft 2in (15.9m) x 30ft 4in (9.25m)
E Tw scr, oil; 4 stroke sgl acting; 12 cyls; 719 NHP; By builder.
H Steel, 3 decks; F: 42ft (12.8m), B: 84ft (25.6m), P: 31ft (9.45m). **P** 12.
1915 Built as *Glenavy*, Glen Line, London.
1924 Acquired by PSNC; renamed *Lagarto*.
1948 Broken up at Troon.

TEMUCO

188 **TEMUCO**

B 1925 Harland & Wolff, Glasgow; **T:**110g, 66n.
D 86ft (26.21m) x 19ft (5.79m) x 9ft 9in (3.02m).
E Sgl scr, oil; 2 stroke sgl acting; 2 cyls; machinery aft.
H Steel, 1 deck.
1925 Tug and water tender at Valparaiso.
1942 Sold locally.

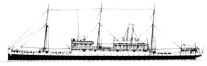

CHAMPERICO

189 **CHAMPERICO**

B 1911 Caledon S.B. Co., Dundee; **T:**2,548g, 1,422n.
D 290ft 1in (88.42m) x 41ft 8in (12.7m) x 17ft (5.18m).
E Sgl scr, tpl exp; 3 cyls; 321 NHP; Stm P: 180 lb; 3 sgl ended boilers, 9 furnaces; 12 kts; By builder.
H Steel, 2 decks; F: 45ft (13.72m), B and P: 197ft (60.05m)
P 100.
1911 Built as *Andorinha* for Yeoward Bros., Liverpool. Employed on Liverpool-Madeira-Canary Isles services.
1917 Acquired by PSNC; renamed *Champerico* and placed on Coastal passenger services along the Peruvian and Central American coasts.
1934 Sold to Torres y Ward Cia, Valparaiso; renamed *Vina del Mar* after the holiday resort adjacent to Valparaiso.
193? Transferred to Chilean State Railways.
1950 Transferred with the State Railways fleet into Empresa Maritima del Estado de Chilena (The State Marine).
1966 (circa) Broken up. The vessel was only classified by Lloyds until 6/1960.

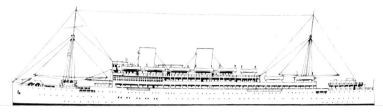

REINA DEL PACIFICO

190 **REINA DEL PACIFICO**

B 1931 Harland & Wolff, Belfast; T:17,702g, 10,720n, 23,500 disp.

D 551ft 4in (168.05m) x 76ft 4in (23.27m) x 37ft 9in (11.51m).

E Quad scr, oil; 4 stroke sgl acting Buchi supercharged; 4 x 12 cyls; 2,844 NHP; 18 kts; By builder.

H Steel, 3 decks; F: 102ft (31.09m), B: 354ft (107.9m), 5 holds. P: 47ft (14.33m)

P 280 1st, 162 2nd, 446 3rd.

1930 Sept 23: launched. PSNC's largest vessel thus far. First white hull and a passenger ship name which did not commence with "O". Fore funnel dummy.

1931 Mar 27: 3 day maiden North Sea shake down cruise with guests.

1931 Apr 9: maiden voyage Liverpool-La Rochelle-Vigo-Bermuda-Bahamas-Havana-Jamaica-Panama Canal-Guayaquil-Callao (19 days)-Antofagasta-Valparaiso (25½ days).

1932 Jan 19: Recommenced the 'Round South America' service, which she undertook once annually.

1936 Made a record passage to Valparaiso in 25 days.

1939 Aug 3: Arrived at Liverpool and sent to Clyde to await orders.

Sept 3: War was declared. Sept 7: Left the Clyde in a convoy of 17 ships for the Far East.

Dec: Made one voyage to Halifax then converted at Liverpool into a troopship.

1940 Apr 11: Left the Clyde with four other troopers for Harstad, Norway. Proceeded to Bygden Fjord. Steamed at full speed in circles for two hours whilst the Fjord was depth charged by her escorts. Bombed unsuccessfully during disembarkation.

May: Returned to Norway to evacuate troops. May 16: West Africa.

July 24: Left for Suez via Cape Town, with R.A.F. personnel. Their Spitfires being aboard the accompanying aircraft carrier *Argus*.

Nov 14: Repeated the Suez voyage.

1941 Jan: Carried the 4th Indian Division from Suez to Port Sudan for Ethiopia.

March: Bombed at Avonmouth, ineffectually, for three successive nights; moved to the Clyde and again bombed but missed.

Mar 22: Loaded with troops struck a submerged object in the Bristol Channel and lost a propeller. Repairs at Liverpool.

Apr 15: Air attacks at Liverpool missed although a delayed action bomb went off, in the water alongside, at breakfast time next day. Left on time with troops for Cape Town.

After a second South African voyage undertook North Atlantic crossings out of Halifax.

Dec 5: Liverpool-Cape Town-Bombay-Colombo-Liverpool.

1942 April 12: Repeated her Bombay voyage.

Aug 6: Made one trip to North America to fetch U.S. and Canadian troops. At Liverpool drydocked and painted. Lifeboats replaced by landing craft.

Sept 13: To the Clyde. There with other troopers commenced practice landing operations.

Oct 17: A full rehearsal for the North African landings was carried out at Loch Linne.

Oct 21: Embarked troops for the 'Z' landing at Oran. She was flagship to Senior Naval

Officer Landing. The Algiers force had to be 24hrs ahead of the Oran force so that at one stage *Reina del Pacifico* had to steam back on her tracks for 8 hours in order to pass through the Straits of Gibraltar in darkness.

Nov 7/8: At 15.30 met up with the equipment ships (on time to the minute). At 20.00 rendez-voused with the marker submarine and by 23.30 was in position. 102 ships were assembled. (it is worth mentioning that a five ship French convoy then came out of Oran but did not give the game away). 07.00: Her landing craft, having joined others in the assembly area, went ashore being 4 minutes early because of shallows through which the troops waded. Later she berthed in Oran harbour.

Nov 24: Back in the Clyde she picked up reinforcements for Algiers.

1945 Jan 5: Took reinforcements to Oran.

May 5: Arrived at Suez to commence practices for the Sicily invasion.

June 29: Embarked the 51st Highland Division

July 10: Landed them at Avola Beach, Sicily. She returned to Malta and then proceeded to Oran to evacuate 500 German prisoners-of-War.

Twice attacked by the Luftwaffe.

July 23: arrived back in the Clyde.

Aug: Carried King Peter of Jugoslavia and his entourage Liverpool-Suez. It was her only voyage free from air attack. Thence to Taranto and Port Augustus with troops. At Sicily she embarked the U.S. First Division H.Q. Staff for Britain for their preparations for the Normandy invasion.

Nov 15: Liverpool-Bombay with troops. The convoy of 20 ships was attacked (Nov 26) by 60 planes. *Delius*, Lamport & Holt was the only loss. On Nov 29 24 JU 88's attacked scoring several hits but no ships were lost.

1944 Jan: Made a trooping voyage to East Africa then spent the next ten months as a Mediterranean troop ferry

Dec: Liverpool-Iceland-New York. This tireless ship then went on Pacific trooping duties until the end of hostilities.

1946 Used as a Repatriation ship. She sailed in all 350,000 miles and carried safely 150,000 men and women of over twenty nationalities.

1947 Jan: Returned to her builders for an overhaul and refit. New furniture was needed because her stored fitments had been destroyed by bombing.

Sept 10: Trials commenced.

Sept 11: An engine room explosion killed 28. The piston in port outer No. 2 engine overheated and the engine blew up.

1948 Reverted to Liverpool-Valparaiso service, a year late.

1957 July 8: Went aground on Devil's Flat, Bermuda. Came off 2 days later with no damage.

Nov: Lost a propeller at Havana. A new one was delivered by *Salinas* (195).

1958 Apr 27: Last voyage. Withdrawn from service; broken up by British Iron & Steel Corp. (John Cashmore) at Newport, Mon.

TALCA (III)

191 TALCA (III)

B 1943 Bethlehem Fairfield Shipyard Inc., Baltimore, Maryland; **T:**7,219g, 4,454n.

D 422ft 9in (128.85m) x 57ft (17.37m) x 34ft 9in (10.59m).

E Sgl scr, tpl exp; 3 cyls; 450 NHP; Stm P: 225lb, 2 watertube boilers; 14 kts; By General Machinery Corp., Hamilton, Ontario.

H Steel, electric welded, 2 decks.
1943 Laid down as *Orville P. Taylor,* completed as *Samothrace,* operated by Royal Mail.
1947 Acquired and renamed *Talca.*
1953 Sold; renamed *Popi,* Cia Naveira Aris SA, Puerto Limon, Costa Rica.
1961 Became *Lydia,* Atlas Maritime Finance Corp., Beirut, Lebanon.
1967 July: Broken up at Whampoa, China.

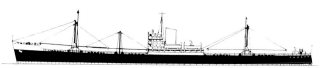

SAMANCO, SARMIENTO (II)

192 **SAMANCO**
B 1943 Harland & Wolff, Belfast; **T:**6,413g, 3,759n.
D 466ft 4in (142.19m) oa, 448ft 2in (136.6m) x 62ft 9in (19.12m) x 34ft 9in (10.59m).
E Sgl scr, oil; 2 stroke direct acting; 8 cyls; 1,643 NHP; 15 kts; By builder.
H Steel, 1 deck and shelter deck; F: 42ft (12.8m).
1943 Aug: Completed.
1951 Oct 17: Collided with *George Uhler,* Prudential S S Co., off Dungeness.
1956 Sold to Deutsche Dampschiff "Hansa"; renamed *Reichenfels.*
1962 Broken up in Spain.

193 **SARMIENTO (II)**
Details as *Samanco* (192) except:- **B** 1945; **T:**6,393g, 3,743n.
1945 Oct: Completed.
1969 Sold to Monomachos Cia Nav. S.A., Piraeus, Greece; renamed *Monomachos.*
1970 Became *Gladiator* owned by Eagle Ocean Shipping Co., Famagusta, Cyprus.
1971 Feb 28: Left Havana for Shanghai and broken up in China.

SALAMANCA, SALINAS, SALAVERRY, SANTANDER

194 **SALAMANCA**
B 1948 Harland & Wolff, Belfast; **T:**6,704g, 3,923n.
D 467ft (142.34m) oa, 440ft (134.11m) x 62ft (18.9m) x 30ft (9.14m).
E Sgl scr, oil; 2 cycle dbl acting; 8 cyls; 1,933 NHP; 13 kts; By builder.
H Steel, 1 deck and shelter deck; F: 42ft (12.8m). **P 12.**
1948 Entered service. The "S" class service was UK-Bermuda-Bahamas-Cuba-Colombia-Panama-Colombia(Pacific)-Ecuador-Peru-Chile.
1967 Sold to El Chaco Cia. Nav. S.A. Piraeus; renamed *Kronos.*
1972 Oct 17: Left Singapore for Shanghai and broken up.

195 SALINAS

Details as *Samanco* (192) except:- **B** 1947; **T:**6,705g, 3,923n.
1947 Nov: Completed.
1956 During the Suez crisis *Salinas* was taken over as a Store ship.
1968 Sold for £160,000 to Polyfimos Cia. Nav, Greece and renamed *Polyfimos.*
1972 Dec 6: Left Singapore for Shanghai for breaking up.

196 SALAVERRY

Details as *Samanco* (192) except:- **B** 1946; **T:**6,647g, 3,879n.
1946 Aug: Completed.
1967 Sold for £150,000 to Detabi Cia Nav., Piraeus, Greece; renamed *Pelias.*
1972 Dec 12: Sank 250 miles south of Durban after springing a leak which flooded the engine room. Maceio-Saigon. All saved.

197 SANTANDER

Details as *Samanco* (192) except:- **B** 1946; **T:**6,648g.
1946 May: Completed.
1967 Sold to Navmachos S.S.Co, Famagusta, Cyprus for £147,500. Renamed *Navmachos.*
1971 Dec 9: Sold for $166,000 and broken up in Spain by Villaneuva y Geltru.

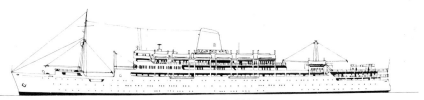

REINA DEL MAR

198 REINA DEL MAR

B 1956 Harland & Wolff, Belfast; **T:**20,750g, 8,260n.
D 600ft 8in (183.09m) oa, 560ft (170.69m) x 78ft 4in (23.88m) x 44ft (13.41m).
E Tw scr, 2 dbl reduction geared Parsons's turbines; 18,700 SHP at 112 r.p.m.; 18 kts; By builder.
H Steel, 3 decks. Denny Brown stabilisers, 5 holds.
P 207 1st, 216 cabin, 343 tourist. Crew: 327.
1955 June 7: Launched.
1956 Apr: Cost £5 million. May 3: maiden voyage Liverpool-Panama Canal-Valparaiso.
1963 Chartered to the Travel Savings Association.
1964 Mar 10: Arrived Belfast for conversion to a cruise liner. **T:** 21,501g; Pass: 1,047 one class. June 10: Placed under Union-Castle Management; first cruise Southampton-New York. Nov: Painted in Union-Castle colours.
1967 T:20,750g.
1969 Transferred to Royal Mail Line ownership.
1973 Sept: Sold to Union-Castle Mail S S Co.
1975 July 30: Arrived Kaohsuing, Taiwan. Broken up by Tung Cheng Steel Co.

KENUTA (II), FLAMENCO (II), POTOSI (IV), PIZARRO (II) COTOPAXI (II)
199 KENUTA (II)

B 1950 Greenock Dockyard Co., Greenock; **T:**8,494g, 4,501n.
D 512ft 7in (156.24m) oa, 488ft 11in (149.02m) x 66ft 4in (20.22m) x 29ft 7in (9.02m).
E Sgl scr, 3 dbl reduction turbines; 10,340 SHP; 16 kts; By Parson's Marine Turbine Co.
H Steel, 1 deck and shelter deck; F: 37ft (11.28m), P:26ft (7.92m) 5 holds; Cargo: 630,000 cu ft (17.829 cu m). **P** 12.
1950 Aug: Completed. Originally laid down for the Clan Line but purchased on the stocks with *Flamenco* (200).
1971 Towed by the tug *Mumbles* to Antwerp for breaking up.

200 FLAMENCO (II)

Details as *Kenuta* (199) except:- **B:** 1950: **T:**8,491g, 4,504n.
1950 Dec: Entered South American PSNC service.
1966 Sold to Cia. de Nav. Abeto S.A.; renamed *Pacific Abeto*.
1982 Broken up at Chittagong.

201 POTOSI (IV)

Details as *Kenuta (199) except:-* **B** 1955; **T:**8,564g, 4,556n.
1955 Feb 23: Launched. South American cargo services.
1972 Sold to Granvias Oceanicos Armadora S.A, Piraeus and renamed *Kavo Pieratis*.
1976 Oct: Sold to W. H. Arnott Young & Co and broken up at Dalmuir.

202 PIZARRO (II)

Details as *Kenuta* (199) except:- **B** 1955; **T:**8,564g, 4,556n.
1955 Oct 14: Maiden voyage round South America cargo service.
1972 Sold to Navieros Progresivos S.A, Piraeus. Renamed *Kavo Maleas*.
1974 Nov: Broken up by Chin Ho Fa Steel & Iron Works, Kaohsiung.

203 COTOPAXI (II)

B 1954 Wm Denny & Co., Dumbarton; **T:**8,559g, 4,552n.
D 512ft 6in (156.21m) oa, 476ft (145.08m) x 66ft 4in (20.22m) x 27ft 11in (8.51m).
E Sgl scr, dbl reduction geared turbine; 9,400 SHP; 2 Babcock & Wilcox boilers; Stm P: 510 lb; 16 kts at 108 r.p.m.; By builder.
H Steel, 1 deck and shelter deck; F: 42ft (12.8m), P: 26ft (7.92m); 5 holds; Cargo: 630,909 cu ft (17,855 cu m) grain. **P** 12.
1954 Apr: Completed.
1973 Sold; renamed *Kavo Longos*, Transportes Mundiales Armadora S.A., Piraeus.
1975 Nov: Broken up in China.

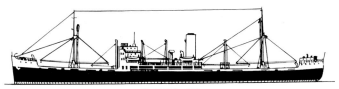

CUZCO (II)

204 CUZCO (II)

B 1951 Blyth Dry Docks & Shipbuilding Co., Blyth; **T:**8,038g, 4,588 n.
D 501ft (152.71m) oa, 481ft 6in (146.76m) x 64ft 2in (19.56m) x 28ft 1in (8.56m).
E Sgl scr, 3 dbl reduction steam turbines; 8,800 SHP; 15½ kts; By Parson's Marine Turbine Co, Wallsend.
H Steel, 2 decks and shelter deck; **F:** 43ft (13.11m), **P:** 38ft (11.58m); Cargo: 754,249 cu ft (21,345 cu m) grain. **P** 12.
1951 Laid down as *Thurland Castle*, James Chambers & Co., Liverpool. Her sister was *Penrith Castle*. Acquired by PSNC and renamed *Cuzco*.
1965 Sold to Wm. Thomson's Benlarig Shipping Co. (Ben Line mgrs) and renamed *Benattow*.
1977 Sept 25: Arrived at Kaohsiung and broken up by Sing Cheng Yung Steel Co.

ELEUTHERA, SOMERS ISLE, CIENFUEGOS/CHANDELEUR

205 ELEUTHERA

B 1959 Hall Russell & Co., Aberdeen; **T:**5,407g, 2,760n.
D 386ft 2in (117.7m) oa, 360ft (109.73m) x 54ft 3in (16.54m) x 25ft 10in (7.87m).
E Sgl scr, oil; 2 stroke sgl acting; 4 cyls; 4,500 BHP; 13½ kts; By Harland & Wolff, Glasgow. **H** Steel, 2 dks. **F:** 38ft (11.58m). **C:**354,000 cu ft (10,018 cu m)g.
1959 May: Entered service.
1970 Laid up in the River Fal. Up for sale.
1971 Became *Mimi-M,* Seahunter Shipping Co, Famagusta.
1974 Sold to Valient Bay Shipping Co, Piraeus; renamed *Maria.*
1984 Nov 1: Arrived at Gadani Beach, Pakistan for breaking up.

206 SOMERS ISLE

Details as *Eleuthera* (205) except:- **B** 1959 Harland & Wolff, Belfast; **T:**5,684g, 2,995n.
D 396ft (120.7m) oa, 370ft (112.78m).
1959 Entered service Bermuda-Caribbean ports-Panama.
1970 Laid up in the River Fal. Up for sale.
1971 Sold to Sealord Shipping Co, Famagusta. Renamed *Eldina.*
1975 Renamed *Commencement,* Commencement Compania Naviera S.A, Famagusta.
1982 Renamed *Caribbean;* same owner.
1983 Became *Melpol,* Commencement Maritime Enterprises, Jersey.
Dec: Damaged by fire in the English Channel enroute Lisbon-Bremen; one lost.
1984 Laid up and finally scrapped.

207 **CIENFUEGOS/CHANDELEUR**

Details as *Eleuthera* (205) except: **T:** 5,224g, 2,760n.

1959 Nov: Entered service as *Cienfuegos.*
1968 Renamed *Chandeleur* by P.S.N.C.; chartered to Royal Mail.
1970 Out of service and up for sale. Laid up in the Fal.
1971 Became *Emma-M,* Seacomber Shipping Co, Famagusta.
1974 Renamed *Lela;* owned by Green Bay Shipping Co, Piraeus.
1981 Sold to the West Asia Shipping Co, Singapore; renamed *Jetpur Viceroy*
1982 Nov 2: Final voyage to Chittagong.
1983 Jan 25: Decommissioned for break-up at Chittagong.

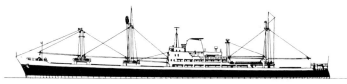

OROYA (IV), ORITA (II), OROPESA (III)

208 **OROYA (IV)**

B 1956 Bremer Vulkan, Vegesack; **T:**6,311g, 3,281n.
D 475ft (144.78m)oa, 440ft (134.11m) x 64ft 4in (19.61m) x 27ft 1in (8.25m).
E Sgl scr, oil, 2 stroke sgl acting; 9 cyls: 30¾in (78cm); Stroke: 55in (140cm).
H Steel, 1 deck and shelter deck; Cargo: 596,825 cu ft (16,890 cu m) grain, 11,000 cu ft (311 cu m) refrigerated.

1956 Built as *Arabic* for Shaw Savill & Albion, London.
1968 Transferred to PSNC; renamed *Oroya.*
1970 Renamed *Pacific Ranger* and operated by Furness Withy.
1971 Reverted to *Oroya.*
1972 Sold to Hong Kong Ocean Shipping Co., Panama; renamed *Lamma Island.*
1983 May 28: Broken up by Inchon Iron & Steel Co, Inchon, Korea.

209 **ORITA (II)**

Details as *Oroya* (208) except:- **B** 1957.

1957 Feb: Built as *Afric* for Shaw Savill & Albion, London.
1968 Transferred to PSNC; renamed *Orita.*
1972 Sold to Hong Kong Islands Shipping Co., Panama; renamed *HongKong Island.*
1983 May 1: Broken up at Inchon, South Korea.

210 **OROPESA (III)**

Details as *Oroya* (208) except:- **B** 1957 Bremer Vulkan, Hamburg; **T:** 6,553g, 3,281n.
1957 Apr: Completed as *Aramaic* for Shaw Savill & Albion, London.
1968 Transferred to PSNC; renamed *Oropesa.*
1970 Renamed *Pacific Exporter* and operated by Furness Withy,
1970 Reverted to *Oropesa.*
1972 Sold to Hong Kong Atlantic Shipping Co., Panama; renamed *Lantao Island.*
1982 Sept 29: Arrived and broken up at Kaohsiung.

WILLIAM WHEELWRIGHT
211 WILLIAM WHEELWRIGHT

B 1960 Harland & Wolff, Belfast; **T:**31,320g, 16,872n.
D 753ft 6in (229.67m) oa, 717ft 9in (218.77m) x 98ft 5in (30m) x 52ft 6in (16m).
E Sgl scr, 2 steam turbines dbl reduction geared; 16,000 SHP; Stm P: 703 lb; 2 water tube boilers 900°F; 16 Kts; By builder.
H Steel, 1 deck; Cargo: 2,097,502 cu ft (59,359 cu m) oil in 26 tanks with 17 bulkheads.
1960 July: Oil Tanker. Registered as owned by Pacific Maritime Services Ltd.
1975 Dec 26: Went aground in ballast off Sinoe, south of Monrovia, Liberia. Dec 29: Refloated; towed to Lisbon but beyond repair. Returned to P.S.N.C. ownership.
1976 Oct: Towed to Santander and broken up by Recuperaciones Submarines S.A.

212 COLOSO

B 1961 A. Hall & Co., Aberdeen; **T:**293g, 176n.
D 101ft (30.78m) oa, 90ft (27.43m) x 26ft 1in (7.95m) x 12ft 8in (3.86m).
E Sgl scr, oil; 2 stroke dbl acting with sgl reduction reversing gear; 8 cyls; 970 BHP; 11 kts; By Ruston & Hornsby, Lincoln.
H Steel, 1 deck.
1961 Tug. Based at Antofagasta. Ownership registered as Servicios Maritimos S.A. Antofagasta, S.A. and flew Chilean flag.
1976 Sold to Ultramar Agencia Maritima, Valparaiso-renamed *Ultramar IV*
1990 Still in service.

GEORGE PEACOCK
213 GEORGE PEACOCK

B 1961 Harland & Wolff, Belfast; **T:**19,153g, 11,307n.
D 643ft 3in (196.06m) oa, 611ft (186.23m) x 80ft 11in (24.66m) x 45ft 6in (13.87m).
E Sgl scr, oil 2 stroke sgl acting; 7 cyls; 11,600 BHP; 15¾ kts; By builder.
H Steel, 1 deck; F: 50ft (15.24m), B: 38ft (11.58m), P: 134ft (40.84m); Cargo: 1,346,454 cu ft (38,105 cu m) oil in 27 tanks.
1961 July: Oil tanker. Registered as owned by Pacific Maritime Services Ltd.
1969 Sold to V. J. Vardinoyannis, Piraeus, Greece; renamed *Georgios V;* **T:**18,798g.
1981 Sold to Varnicos (Varnima Corp); Same name and port.
1985 Still recorded as being in service but laid up.
1990 Still in service.

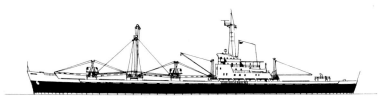

214 ORCOMA (II)
B 1966 Harland & Wolff, Belfast; **T:**10,300g, 3,984n, 14,614 dwt.
D 508ft 9in (155.12m) obb, 480ft (146.3m) x 70ft 2in (21.38m) x 27ft 11in (8.51m).
E Sgl scr, oil; 2 sgl acting B & W type; 8 cyls; 18 kts; 2 Harland & Wolff auxiliary boilers; Stm P: 110 lbs; By builder.
H Steel, 2 dks. F: 50ft (15.24m). Refrig 15,520 cu m. The centre section of the hull from vertical marks on the white strake was whale backed with the bulwarks set back by one metre.
1966 Built for Furness Withy's subsidiary Nile Steamship Co. and chartered to P.S.N.C. for 20 years.
1970 Served as a British Exhibition ship.
1971 Reverted to normal services to South America.
1979 Oct: Sold to P. T. Samudera, Indonesia; renamed *Ek Daya Samudera*.
1984 Mar 31: Arrived at Kaohsiung for demolition by Tai Yuan Steel & Iron Co.

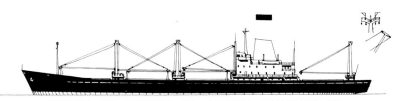

ORBITA (II), ORDUNA (II), ORTEGA (II)/ANDES (II)

215 ORBITA (II)
B 1972 Cammell Laird & Co., Birkenhead; **T:**8,396g, 4,302n.
D 529ft 8in (161.45m) oa, 501ft 10in (152.97m) x 73ft 4in (22.36m) x 44ft (13.42m).
E Sgl scr, oil 2 stroke sgl acting; 8 cyls; type 8K74EF: 13,720 BHP; 18 kts; Burmeister & Wain type; By J. G. Kincaird & Co. Unmanned engine room.
H Steel, 2 decks; F: 47ft 3in (14.4m).
Cargo: 858,869 cu ft (24,306 cu m) grain. Accommodates 300 x 20ft containers.
1972 Built for P.S.N.C. which was now a part of the Royal Mail Division of Furness Withy. Operated by P.S.N.C. out of Liverpool.
1980 Apr: Sold to Cia. Sud Americana de Vapores, Valparaiso. Renamed *Andalien*.
1980 Sold to Wallem & Co, Hong Kong, renamed *Morning Sun*.
1980 Returned to Sud Americana. Renamed *Rubens*.
1990 Still in service.

216 ORDUNA (II)
Details as *Orbita* (215) except:- B 1973.
1973 March: Completed for the South American services.
1980 Registered as owned by Royal Mail Line with P.S.N.C. as managers.
1982 Sept 30: Became *Beacon Grange* of the Furness Withy Shipping.

1984 Sold to Cenargo Ltd, the building contractor for the Falkland Islands airport. Employed carrying materials from UK to Port Stanley. *Merchant Pioneer.*
1990 Still in service.

217 ORTEGA (II)/ANDES (II)

Details as *Orbita* (215) except: **B** 1973.
1973 July: Completed.
1980 Apr: Renamed *Andes.* Registered as owned by Royal Mail Line but operated by P.S.N.C. out of Liverpool.
1982 Aug: Renamed *Oceanhaven.* Owned by Blue Haven Co. Ltd, Hong Kong.
1987 Renamed Kota Akbar by Pacific International Lines (Pte) Ltd. Present fleet.

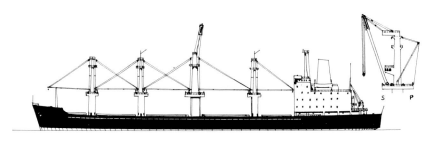

OROYA (V) OROPESA (IV)

218 OROYA (V)

B 1978 Lithgows Ltd., Port Glasgow; **T**:9,015g, 5,529n.
D 535ft 3in (163.15m) oa, 508ft 7in (155m) x 75ft 4in (22.97m) x 44ft (13.42m).
E Sgl scr, oil 2 stroke sgl acting; 6 cyls; 12,000 BHP; 16¼ kts. Sulzer type by Scotts Eng. Co., Greenock.
H Steel, 2 decks; F: 39ft (11.9m).
1978 Apr: Entered P.S.N.C. service but registered as owned by Ardgowan Shipping Co., London; Furness Withy Shipping as manager.
1985 Transferred to Shaw, Savill & Albion. Same name.
1986 R/n *Yinka Folawiyo,* Nigerian Green Lines, Lagos.
1989 Sold to Cenargo Ltd. R/n *Merchant Premier.* Managers: V Ships (UK) Ltd. Present fleet.

219 OROPESA (IV)

Details as *Oroya* (218). Superstructure windows: 3 dks x 4 pairs.
1978 Apr: Entered P.S.N.C. service but the ship was shown as being owned by Blackhall Shipping Co.
1982 Operated by Shaw, Savill & Albion out of Liverpool.
1984 May 25: Sold at the same time as *Orduña* (216) to Cenargo Ltd and placed on Falkland Islands service. *Merchant Principal.*
1990 Still in service.

ANDES (III)

220 **ANDES (III)**

B 1984 Hyundai Heavy Industries Co, Ulsan, S. Korea. **T:**32,150g, 18,016n, 37,900 dwt.

D 662.7ft (202m) oa, 626ft (190.8) x 105.6ft (32.2m) x 61.6ft (18.8m). Dft: 39.3ft.

E Sgl scr, oil, 5 cyl B & W type 5L90 GBE, 19,300 BHP, 18½ kts. By builder.

H Steel. 2 dks. Bow thruster. Crew 24.

C: 2145 TEU's Holds 2, 3, 4 and 6 equipped for bulk copper with TEU's over. Hold 1: Dangerous cargoes. Hold 5: Refrigerated; 254 TEU's for bananas. All holds are strengthened for fork lift trucks.

1 x 40 ton O & K gantry crane railed to all forward holds.

1983 Nov 16: Launched for Furness, Withy; placed with PSNC.

1984 Built to operate as one of seven ships on the Eurosal (Europe South America Line) service. *Andes* being the Furness Withy member. These containerships replaced 28 conventional freighters. The self unloading gantry is provided for use at ports without container cranes.

1990 Still in service.

CHARTERED

ALBEMARLE, WALSINGHAM

220 **ALBEMARLE**

B 1950 Burntisland S.B. Co., Burntisland; **T:**3,364g, 1,574n.

D 364ft 9in (111.18m) oa, 348ft 8in (106.27m) x 51ft 2in (15.6m) x 18ft 7in (5.66m).

E Sgl scr, oil; 2 stroke sgl acting; 4 cyls; 3,300 BHP; 14 kts; By Hawthorn Leslie & Co., Newcastle.

H Steel, 1 deck and shelter deck; F: 30ft (9.14m), B: 100ft (30.48m). **P** 12.

1950 Built as *Afric* for Prince Line (Furness Withy) placed in Shaw Savill & Albion service.

1955 Transferred to PSNC; renamed *Albermarle*. The ships were actually chartered. Placed on an experimental service between Bermuda-Caribbean Ports-Panama.

The experiment led to the building of three ships *Cienfuegos* (207) *Eleuthera* (205) and *Somer's Isle* (206).

1957 Transferred back to Prince Line; renamed *Scottish Prince*.

1968 Sold; renamed *Grigorios*. Klimnos Shipping Co, Cyprus.

1972 Purchased by Milos S S Co., Cyprus; renamed *Milos*.

1975 Became *Nestor* II, same owner.

1977 Dec 23: arrived at Gadani Beach, Karachi, for breaking up.

221 **WALSINGHAM**

Details as *Albemarle* (221) except:- **T:**3,343g, 1,519n.

D 363ft (110.64 oa.)

E By D. Rowan & Co., Glasgow.
1950 Feb: Built as *Sycamore* for Johnston Warren Lines (Furness Withy)
1955 Chartered to PSNC with her sister for the same routes: renamed *Walsingham.*
1957 Reverted to *Sycamore* and Johnston Warren service.
1966 Transferred to Prince Line management; renamed *Merchant Prince.*
1968 Became *Elias L,* Kaldelion Shipping Co., Limassol.
1975 Sold to Melteco Navigation Ltd, Limassol; renamed *Meltemi.*
1978 Her name was shortened to *Temi* by her new owners, Green Spirit Inc, Limassol.
1979 May 10: Arrived at Gadani Beach for breaking up.

SAILING SHIPS

222 ELIZABETH
B 1832 Bristol; **T:**445 **E** Sailing ship. **H** Wood.
1835 Built for Miles & Co., Bristol for Jamaica service.
1840 Jan: Acquired by PSNC to carry coal to Valparaiso and then to be converted into a coal hulk.
The crew claimed that the ship was unsuited to the voyage round Cape Horn and refused to sail in her.
1840 Feb: Sold.
Note: 105 *Elizabeths* are in Lloyds Register for 1840.

223 PORTSEA
B 1808 Calcutta; **T:**451. **E** Sailing barque. **H** Wood.
1808 Built for London-Calcutta trade.
1840 Feb: Acquired by PSNC to replace *Elizabeth* (223).
Became a coal hulk at Valparaiso. Topmasts and yards removed. Disposal date not known.

224 CECILIA
B 1815 Dunbar; **T:**325 **E** Sailing barque
1815 Built for Alexander & Co., Glasgow. Clyde-Australia service.
1841 Acquired by PSNC for use as a coal hulk at Valparaiso. Topmasts and yards removed. Took out a cargo of coal.

225 JASPER
No details traced.
1841 Became a coal hulk on the South American station. Sailed with coal to Valparaiso but not necessarily hulked at that port.